Profitable Technology Services Pricing

How to use offering design and pricing
strategy to accelerate sales and
increase willingness to pay

Timothy Matanovich

VALUE AND PRICING PARTNERS

tsia | SERVICES EXCELLENCE
ALLIANCE PARTNER

tsia | RECOGNIZED
INNOVATOR
INNOVATION IN CONSULTING
WINNER BEST PRACTICES 2012

Advance Praise for
Profitable Technology Services Pricing

"Read your book. FABULOUS. Seriously. I learned a lot and thought it was very well written and I would never have thought I would have said that about a pricing book."
- **Randy Wootton, Vice President, Premier Success Plans, Salesforce.com**

"The book definitely got my attention. You have opened new ways of thinking about how to position our offerings moving forward as well as creating new offerings."
- **Christophe Bodin, VP & GM, Customer Support, ESM BMC Software**

"Timothy Matanovich relegates some pretty complex theory and economic models into ideas and concepts that are easily understood by the lay person. The book starts by educating one on the marked differences between cost based, market based and value based pricing. Once the initiation is completed, the author constantly brings one back to re-visit these approaches to pricing ensuring that the comparison between value based pricing versus cost and market based pricing is made throughout the book. I personally appreciated the use of the pricing surfboard framework, and once the book is published, have no doubt that I will be using it in practical implementation going forward. Definitely food for thought. The introduction and detailed explanation of the TS Pricing Strategy framework then elegantly pulls the early chapters together into the more practical and essential part of the book, both from the supplier and customer perspective. Tim draws from his experiences as a pricing strategist to explain in lay terms what could take one years to learn."
- **Farhad Khan, Executive, Enterprise Business Unit, MTN**

"I'm loving it!"
- **Brad Smith, EVP, Customer Experience & Interim CMO, Sage Software, North America**

"In Business-to-Business Markets, Value-Based Pricing is the most important signal you send to your customers – and your competitors and the rest of the market. In this thoroughly thought through system, Tim Matanovich tackles the 'how to's' for what is becoming the most important of these markets –and often the most difficult to navigate –technical services. A clear 'must read' for any one in services marketing."

- **Ralph A. Oliva, Executive Director, Institute for the Study of Business Markets, Professor of Marketing, Smeal College of Business, Penn State University**

"On a topic as mundane as maintenance pricing, Tim has turned it into a strategy for expanding revenue. Worth the read for all those who set prices, create new programs, and determine strategy, but forget to think about sound pricing."

- **Mary Trick, Senior Vice President Maintenance, Infor**

"Determining effective Service & Support pricing is emerging as an essential skill for High Tech Companies. Tim's PTSP System is a clear and practical approach that provides what we need to succeed."

- **Ron Howe, SVP Global Service & Support, Harmonic Inc.**

"As we increasingly find ourselves living 'in the Cloud', Support and Services play an increasingly significant role in driving a company's top line revenue and profitability. Getting pricing right and going beyond traditional 'cost plus' approaches will be critical in this business landscape. Great read, BTW, thanks for sharing."

- **Bryan Belmont, GM, WW Premier Support, Microsoft**

"As product life cycles shorten, service based differentiation becomes vital for revenue growth. Tim's book lays out a clear, concise framework for valuing, packaging and pricing services."

- **Roland Schweyer, VP Samsung Enterprise (Germany)**

"In his book, Tim Matanovich treats pricing as a science, not an art. That's how it should be. Systems thinking makes for successful execution and performance results."

- **Matt Kelly, Vice President, Strategy Software**

"Clear thinking and strategic direction on service pricing are rare indeed. Tim has provided both in this book. It will be a valuable resource for those who seek to profitably grow their businesses through service."

- **Mary Jo Bitner, Executive Director, Center for Services Leadership, W. P. Carey School of Business, Arizona State University**

"Technology services are critical not only for customer satisfaction and retention, but also because they can be extremely profitable. Tim's book is a tremendous resource, providing the most comprehensive coverage I have seen."

- **Tim Andreae, VP of Marketing, Vistaar Technologies**

"Tim lays out an effective approach for expanding how a tech company can price services. As we look to expand our services portfolio, we can draw from Tim's PTSP system to evolve our pricing models and drive more value for our customers and our business..."

- **Dan Walkowski, Vice President, Global Services, Zebra Technologies Corporation**

"With this book Timothy Matanovich closes the missing link between selling the value of your solution and reaping the benefits for your efforts. A must read for all sales forces that have spent heavily on selling value training only to learn that they cannot defend their value proposition facing the purchasing organization of their customers."

- **Andreas Goldman, Partner, New Leaf Partners**

"Historically a tactical and ad hoc approach to pricing has worked for technology services. In the future, however, the lack of strategic pricing could cost companies dearly. Tim's system brings services pricing into the 21st century."

- **Jean Claude Larreche, Alfred H. Heineken Chaired Professor of Marketing, INSEAD**

"Tim Matanovich's new book comes at a critical time. In a sector (technology services) that is seeing dramatic changes (think SaaS) with customers challenging common (and highly profitable) industry pricing practices, Tim guides the reader on how to navigate these changes. With solid research, he makes a compelling case for the power of value-based pricing and its direct link to superior profits. Tim's writing style is engaging and peppered with current examples and insights. In a concise format, he addresses both the strategic and execution sides of value-based pricing, using practical frameworks and tips. I highly recommend this book not only to pricing professionals but also to any technology service executive who is serious about increasing profits while delivering customer value."

- **Philippe Latapie, Partner and Managing Director, StratX**

"As companies in technology industries transition their core of business models from solutions-centric into service-centric models, a pragmatic approach to price services becomes a vital function. Companies cannot get it wrong! In this book, Tim presents a pragmatic and well defined process to tackle the challenge of pricing services by value. The PSTP model is simple, practical an applicable to most services environments. Tim clearly explains the dynamics and forces behind value pricing and the principle of his model, making it easier for Service Managers and Business Executives to evaluate and execute their service pricing transition"

- **Fernando Amendola, Sr. Product Manager , Video Cloud Solution, Cisco Systems**

"The book provides a thoughtful, yet practical approach to developing and evolving pricing strategies. A must read, and a guide for any services leader tasked with valuing and pricing offerings."

- **Brian Hodges, SVP Global Professional Services, Informatica**

"If James Bond were a pricer, this would be Q's briefcase of gadgets served with a martini, shaken, not stirred."

- **Dan Spirek, Executive Vice President and Chief Strategy and Marketing Officer, TriZetto**

For Sean and Alex,
These are my beloved sons in whom I am well pleased

In memory of my dad, John Matanovich.
May I be the craftsman in my work that he was in his

For all our wounded warriors
Thank you for all you have given and continue to give

Table of Contents

Forward

By Thomas Lah

Coauthor of *Consumption Economics*

Executive Director, The Technology Services Industry Association

Historically, technology companies have enjoyed wonderful margins from their service businesses. For the past eight years, I have been tracking the quarterly public results of fifty of the largest technology solution providers on the planet. On average, these companies now enjoy service margins over fifty-percent. Beneath the public data that blends the margins of all service lines together, we know that there are some product companies enjoying margins well north of eighty-percent on their maintenance and support service offerings. These service margin dollars have become critical to the economic engines of product companies. However, these wonderful service margins are now at great risk.

My colleagues and I at The Technology Services Industry Association believe the following realities will dramatically impact the future of service pricing by technology companies:

- Product companies will face immense pricing pressure on service offerings that are required to stand up and maintain a technology environment.
- These traditional service revenue streams will be declining.
- To offset decline in demand, service organizations will need to identify new service offerings.
- To offset pricing pressure, service organizations will need to revise service pricing models.
- As customers migrate to consumption based pricing models for technology, they will push for "value realization" pricing mechanisms for services.

Unfortunately, the service pricing practices of companies in the technology industry are ill prepared to face these realities. Historically, technology companies have pursued two pricing approaches for their service offerings:

1. Percentage Of: Charge customers a percentage of the product price (support service pricing model)

2.   Cost Plus: Determine the cost to deliver the service and place a target margin on top of that cost.

These two pricing models will not serve technology companies well in the future. Technology companies will have to become much more sophisticated and nuanced in their service pricing practices. And that is where Tim enters the discussion.

Profitable Technology Services Pricing is a book that introduces concepts that all service managers will soon need to embrace. This is the first book I have read that helps service organizations think through their pricing practices in a very structured way--and in a way to that asks the right questions for today's service pricing realities. Tim has an intense passion for creating service pricing that aligns with value. This is a passion that all technology providers will soon need to share. Tim has created a body of work that helps technology companies reengineer their pricing practices to align with the customer expectations of today.

There is a coming storm that has the potential to devastate the margins of service organizations that are centered by technology products. This book is a life raft to keep your technology service margins and profits afloat in that storm.

Thomas Lah

"May you live in interesting times."
- Chinese Curse

CHAPTER 1 - AN INCREDIBLY INTERESTING SANDBOX

This book is premised on the supposition that technology services are different, certainly different than technology products and different even from pure services, and therefore merit their own approach to pricing. Technology services are those services that permit each one of us, in hundreds, perhaps thousands, of ways daily, to benefit from the exponential growth in the capabilities of technology. In medicine, communications, information processing, automation, or a myriad of other industries, these technologies permit us to live healthier and longer, create more powerful social relationships, land the *Curiosity* rover on Mars, create a smart power grid that minimizes the incidence of blackouts, and maybe, just maybe, will help us minimize the adverse consequences of global warming.

But why pricing? Because there is a fundamental shift occurring in what services are valued, how they are valued, and the mechanisms by which they are paid for. Cost based pricing and market based pricing, the staples of technology services, are becoming less relevant daily as demand shifts from essential to value added services. Value based pricing, once viewed as an unnecessary luxury, may become essential to the financial success of technology service businesses.

But value based pricing capabilities are only one part of the solution. If we are to have a pricing system, that works day in and day out in a technology services environment, across all technology services, in a period of discontinuous innovation and change, then that system must successfully meet the challenges of the 21st century technology environment.

LET'S START WITH SOFTWARE

At some point in the distant past a manager inside a software company made an absolutely brilliant decision. The name of the individual is lost to history, but the brilliance cannot be denied. It was simple really, and necessary. When we install our software onto the company's hardware, he reasoned, the software will work perfectly. From there, it's all downhill. Over time, the company will change their requirements. They will upgrade their hardware and expect our software to continue working. They will want our software to talk to other software. They will change processes, and new best practices will emerge. The user base will evolve. Each of these changes will decrease the usefulness of our software to the customer.

Of necessity we need to continually upgrade and maintain our software so it continues to deliver the value promised, but how do we pay for it? He made the decision to charge customers 20% per year of the initial license price to cover these costs. In this moment, this manager gave birth to maintenance revenues. The rest is history. Maintenance is arguably the single most profitable revenue source inside software companies. With margins approaching 80%, it is a gold mine. And it is a mine that churns out those profitable revenues year in and year out. For at least three decades, maintenance revenues have been the mother's milk of software companies, the gift that keeps on giving.

But Houston, we have a problem. A new cadre of competitors is emerging, offering software as a service. By hosting the software themselves, they can eliminate much of the complexity that justifies maintenance payments. More, the capex software investment by corporate IT, requiring board approval, is becoming an opex decision by a business unit head. Maintenance? What's that? With remarkably low costs for trial and low risk in implementation, as of this writing demand for SaaS solutions is growing exponentially.

The era of software maintenance may be coming to a close, and established players in the enterprise software industry have arguably the biggest pricing headache in the history of the world. This is the single biggest pricing problem any industry has faced since the early 2000s when Business Week proclaimed "The China Price" as the three most terrifying words in business. Perhaps today, the terror is in "The SaaS Price".

> *Established players in the enterprise software industry have potentially the biggest pricing headache in the history of the world: The SaaS price.*

But the demise of maintenance revenues is only the tip of the iceberg. What is the need for millions of highly skilled technology professional services people, when implementation work decreases to a fractions of its former glory? The problem more broadly is essential services. The services that have contributed so much to the growth and profitability of software companies have largely been essential services. Put simply, they are essential because the software simply would not function if not for these services. Therein is the services pricing problem. Implementation and maintenance permit the product value to be realized, but offer little value in their own right. Their prices are a necessary evil customers are willing to pay to ensure the value of the software is delivered.

That's why cost based and market based pricing models have worked for essential services. Historically, no matter which software supplier customers chose, implementation and maintenance services were a necessary part of the equation. In this world, how are proserve rates justified? Well, those are the rates everybody pays for these services. These are our costs or these are the market rates, so you should pay them. Similarly, why should companies pay 20% of the product price for maintenance? Answer: That is what all software companies charge. It's not our fault. This is the market price, so you should pay it.

But the competitive game is changing. If customers can get the software value with little implementation and maintenance service investment, they will do so in a heartbeat. In this brave new world, essential services are no longer essential. Willingness to pay, therefore, disappears. That's not to say that maintenance revenues will disappear overnight. Depending on your competitive situation, they could last a decade. But the end game is clear. So if software companies are going to maintain their services revenue streams, then they must transition to value added services. These are services that have value in their own right, beyond the software value.

BEYOND SOFTWARE

More broadly in technology markets, service revenue streams are facing new challenges and opportunities. Many companies are facing challenges with the "as a Service" price. Look up Cloud Computing on Wikipedia and you will find 14 XaaS models from Infrastructure as a Service to Backend as a Service. What is the need for a field service force if hardware is delivered as a service?

Other forces are at play as well. For example, if your latest generations of technology are incorporating self diagnostics, and diagnostics have been an important role of your service team's value prop, then redefining the value prop and pricing accordingly are necessary to maintain service revenues and margins. If your services prices have been tied to your hardware prices and hardware prices are falling, then service margins are in jeopardy. Service margins are often more sensitive to price changes than product margins.

Despite the challenges, whatever the technology and its benefits, smart people are needed to make it work. Hmmm, perhaps that sentence understates their contribution. Let's try this. Smart people are needed to make these technologies, largely incomprehensible to most of us, work to solve our problems and enable our futures. Smart people are needed to make the technologies sing and dance. These are value added services, services that have value in their own right. These are services that have unique value to groups of customers or even to a single customer. The one size fits all service and pricing model of maintenance does not apply.

The role of services is changing. Historically managing and solving systems issues were a critically important service role. Now consider Salesforce.com. You can have a CRM for $5 per month per person. If I am a sales VP interested in upgrading my CRM, the services I am interested in are those related to the productivity of my sales people, selling my products and services, in my industry. If there are systems problems, I assume Salesforce.com will handle them behind the scenes. I don't have to worry about them and I certainly don't expect to pay for them.

STRATEGIC, VALUE BASED PRICING

To make money with services in this new world, service value must be demonstrated and documented. When services are not essential, customers don't need to buy. The necessary evil pitch won't work. But by demonstrating and documenting value added by services, customers will want to buy to further their own self interest. Services move from being a part of the customer's cost stream to being part of their success stream. These are services where value pricing simply makes sense. Value pricing is an organizational belief system with the core tenet that price should be based on the economic impact of a service on the customer's business, i.e. the economic value delivered, relative to competitive alternatives.

The shift from cost based and market based pricing to value based pricing is also a shift from pricing tactically to pricing strategically. In *Complexity Avalanche*, the author refers to a question posed by the CIO of Computer Sciences Corporation. "I know how to improve operating efficiencies in services, but how do I make strategic investments there?"[1] Strategic pricing provides an answer to this question. Strategy is fundamentally about resource allocation. The answer to the question, from a strategic pricing perspective, is to invest in services where value is high, providing high incentives for customers to buy and permitting us to capture a fair share of that value for revenues and profits.

---

[1] J.B. Wood, Complexity Avalanche: Overcoming the Threat to Technology Adoption

This answer may appear trite, but in this context we are not talking about the term value as it is bandied about in business circles with the definition changing from conversation to conversation and with no ability to measure or quantify. Rather I am using the term value as defined by leading value researchers Anderson and Narus.[2] *"Value in business markets is the worth in monetary terms of the technical, economic, service and social benefits a customer receives in exchange for the price it pays for a market offering."*

So the answer to the CIO's question is to invest in those services that have the greatest measurable monetary impact on the business model of the buyer. These services will appeal most strongly to the customer and, in turn, permit you to charge a value based price. Indeed, value based pricing is ultimately about being paid fairly for delivering high business impact.

And business impact is the name of the game. Demonstrating business impact can be instrumental in making services value tangible. After developing an economic value model for a firm selling broadband

> *How should service leaders make strategic investments in services? Invest in those services that have the greatest economic impact on the business model of the buyer. Then set a price that permits you to capture a fair share of that value delivered.*

telecommunication services, the CIO remarked that "It's a license for printing

---

[2] James C. Anderson and James A. Narus, Business Market Management: Understanding, Creating and Delivering Value, 2nd ed.,

money." After the firm closed a sizable sale with the State of Wisconsin, the state purchasing agent remarked "Yours was the only vendor that demonstrated why this investment makes sense for our state."

Pricing strategically is about changing the question from an internal orientation where costs are the driver to an external orientation where customer value is the driver. The question changes from "What price do I need to cover my costs and achieve my revenue objectives?" to "What price is the customer willing to pay for the services, and what costs should I incur to deliver them?" The difference is subtle, but the business consequences can be profound. [3]

Pricing strategically, therefore, has direct implications for the services engineering process. Cost based pricing puts pricing at the end of the process. Pricing strategically puts pricing at the front of the process. At the front it drives the firm to eliminate unnecessary costs early in the development process and focuses development on service attributes the customer is willing to pay for -- a wicked good combination for creating both competitive advantage and high margins.

Pricing strategically simplifies the complexity in offering design. It drives attention of the customer, sales organization, and development team away from features and functions (complex) and toward how those features and functions combine to deliver improved business performance (simple).

Cost based pricing needlessly exposes the firm to two risks. The first risk is that the firm builds a service operation with a cost structure that the customer

---

[3] Thomas Nagle and Reed Holden, The Strategy and Tactics of Pricing

cannot afford. The second risk occurs because of the margin target orientation. Instead of exploring the pricing upside, the firm settles for a target margin return, forever losing potential value it could have captured. Alternatively pricing strategically leads the firm to scale the service offering to meet customer demand and positions the firm for higher margins.

The outcome of market based pricing may even be worse. If you indeed have unique value to your customers, then pricing similar to the competition leads directly to needless price competition. Your higher value prompts your competitor to drop price in order to stay in the game. Whammo! You started a price war and didn't even know it. In truth, Pogo was right: "We have discovered the enemy, and he is us". Experience across a wide variety of industries confirms that most price competition is unintentional and unnecessary. Further, most of the harm resulting from price competition is self inflicted.

The strategic pricing process can be summarized in five steps.

The Strategic Pricing Process

1. Identify the <u>target</u> customer or segment.

2. Quantify the <u>value</u> to the customer of solving their problem.

3. Determine the <u>price</u> the customer would be willing to pay to solve the problem.

4. Determine the service <u>offering</u> and cost structure needed to deliver the expected value.

5. Decide desired demand for the service given business and financial objectives.

In my experience firms who employ the strategic pricing process in offering development find it easier to pick winners from losers, and they are more inclined to make the necessary investments across the board that assure launch success.

DEVELOPING NEW PRICING CAPABILITIES

As companies respond to the pricing challenges described and transition from essential to value added services, pricing moves from an afterthought to an essential skill set. Many service organizations will find that skill set sorely lacking. Investment in pricing capabilities will therefore be required to sustain financial performance. The following exhibit summarizes the changes taking place in pricing.

TS Pricing Evolution

From	To
• Service value follows and extends life of product value	• Service value may lead product value and grow utilization
• Service price piggybacks on product price	• Service price stands alone, based on value delivered
• Few essential service offerings, "one size fits all"	• Many value added services targeting customer segments
• Objective: Sustain core service revenues	• Objectives: Maximize margins of a service portfolio
• Operate as a Cost Center, delivering minimal acceptable value	• Operate as a Profit Center, investing in high ROI services to maximize realized value
• Pricing capabilities are nice to have	
• Reliance on Cost Based or Market Based Pricing	• Pricing capabilities are essential
	• Transition to Value Based Pricing
Services as a Necessity	**Services as Growth Engine**

Copyright 2013 Timothy Matanovich

In sum, the role of pricing in services will rise, driven by changing business economics, deterioration of core maintenance and services, and a broader offering mix. These changes will drive service organizations to beef up pricing capabilities to meet the challenges.

MANAGING THE COMPLEXITY

Developing a value based pricing culture, working through the strategic pricing process and developing pricing capabilities are certainly steps in the right direction. Unfortunately, they are not enough. Here is the problem. There is a level of complexity in technology services pricing that is unmatched anywhere else in the business world.

Let's come back to our old friend software as a point of reference. Software companies will have a flagship product, usually the product that made the company. There will be a perpetual license pricing model built for that product that specifies price level, how that price scales with value, e.g. number of users, and the portion of the product price charged for maintenance. If a term license is needed, it is built from the core model. If a new product is launched, it is typically priced using the same model. If there is to be a hosted price, it will be based off the same model. If there is a SaaS price, again built from the same model. If there is bundle pricing, it is built from the same model. The company's pricing model may be a spreadsheet with 150 pages, but fundamentally the pricing scheme is simple.

Prices for other products may even be simpler. Three routers cost X. Twenty two hubs cost Y. Sixty seven blade servers cost Z. Product pricing in the main is simple. Bundling adds complexity, and so do system sales. Build to spec adds more, but still straightforward.

Now let's look at services. There are professional services customized for a single customer, or there is packaged PS. There are maintenance services and service level agreements. There are training services and field services. There are managed services. The following chart shows the range of technology services as outlined by TSIA.[4]

---

[4] Technology Services Industry Association. www.tsia.com

The TSIA Services Continuum

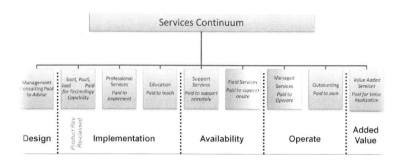

Copyright 2013, Timothy Matanovich

Unlike software or hardware products where the same basic pricing model can be leveraged again and again and again, each service type has unique pricing requirements, requiring a distinct approach to pricing. Implementation, integration and field service may require T&M pricing at market rates. Maintenance requires pricing as a percent of the software price. SLAs may be priced based on hardware or software price, or independent of the product entirely. Training may be bundled into the product sale or sold as a value added service. Managed services may be priced to achieve a set of KPIs and include a gain share mechanism. Systems or solution sales may include products, packaged services and professional services, all priced for value. With packaged services, pricing is managed like product pricing by product management. With solution sales, pricing is established during the sales process and negotiated by sales with the customer.

A pricing system that works in technology services must have the flexibility to accommodate this variety. More it must include a simple framework that helps the pricing manager to quickly sort through the complexity and decide on the right approach.

Complexity has one more dimension: a rapidly changing technology environment. To some, reading this may seem like a statement of the obvious, a redundancy. For others, the last 30 years have been a period of relative stability compared to what lies ahead. The key point I want to make here is that it doesn't matter which view of the future you subscribe to. If there is anything we can learn from the history of tech, it is that the future is full of surprises.

On the one hand, the world of technology has been defined by complexity. Yet that complexity has resulted in elegantly simple solutions like the iPad, the Nook or the Kindle. Similarly the shift from traditional tech sales to

It was 1996, and I was in the Pit at Crotonville. GE's management development center in New York. I was teaching a course in marketing strategy, but all classes broke because Jack Welch was here to meet with the troops. This was my third time seeing him in this environment, and there was always a nugget of wisdom to be gained.

After about 30 minutes, a manager raised his hand with a question. He introduced himself and began to ask his question. He was obviously nervous, and started to ramble. Before he could finish, Welch held up a hand for him to stop. Then Welch said "Look, it's not rocket science. It's just business." With that, he addressed the core issue and moved on.

tech as a service is a shift from complexity to simplicity in one sense, but also a shift from a simple to more complex business models at the same time. The competitive landscape is changing, pitting traditional powerhouses like Microsoft and Barnes and Noble against newcomers Google and Amazon. Discontinuous innovation surrounds us.

And there are other changes. The purchasing process is changing. We see a shift in decision making. Historically, the technical complexity of the purchase put enormous power in the hands of the CIO. That power is likely to remain a strong force, but the role of functional business leaders and even end users is growing. That shift is fragmenting the sales process, changing the fundamental economics of tech businesses and creating conflicting demands for sophistication and ease of use.

Risk is shifting from the customer to the supplier. Consumption economics may turn the economics of the tech businesses on its head.[5] Instead of 80% of revenues captured at the front end of the customer life cycle, revenues become back loaded as end users choose the services they want to consume. This shift, where it occurs, will put enormous financial pressure on tech companies

The ecosystem itself is changing. In some cases, demand for the ability to configure solutions and build integrated systems will grow. Alternatively, tech as a service may reduce the role of channel partners who have specialized in implementation and integration.

---

[5] J.B. Wood, Todd Hewlin, Thomas Lah, Consumption Economics: The New Rules of Tech

Finally we have to ask about the future of tech services as we have historically known them. Traditional tech services have been essential services. The shift to value added services is not evolutionary, it is revolutionary. Service organizations may very well need to transition from a customer support mindset to a strategic marketing mindset; from a customer service mindset to a sales mindset. This is a sizable cultural shift. Further, products are laying claim to the services moniker. Technology as a service raises the question: Exactly what are services, anyway?

Whatever the outcome, one thing is certain: the future will be full of surprises. The implication for pricing is that it is vital to focus on fundamentals. We can't know the exact pricing problem we will be called on to solve. We can, however, develop strong fundamental pricing capabilities that will deliver financial performance and serve us well no matter the challenge we are facing.

A System for Profitable Technology Services Pricing

This book is titled Profitable Technology Services Pricing, or PTSP. This is a system for improving the quality of pricing decisions in a technology services environment. I am not going to claim to provide solutions to every technology services pricing challenge. Rather we will provide a process for pragmatically addressing pricing threats and opportunities, in a very challenging environment, day in and day out.

In this chapter we have outlined the five necessary requirements of that system.

1. It must facilitate a transition to value based pricing without abandoning cost based and market based approaches where those approaches work well enough.

2. Pricing must move from a tactical necessity at the end of the marketing decision process, to a strategic necessity at the front end of the process.

3. Pricing capabilities will move from a nice to have luxury to a central part of daily business decision making.

4. The system must accommodate the broad range of services in the technology services environment and provide a framework for quickly managing that complexity.

5. Finally, it must be focused on building fundamental skills. The range of potential pricing challenges is too broad to anticipate. The only path to effective price management is to build strong core skills that can be applied proactively, day in and day out.

CLOSING THOUGHT

If you are looking for A Course in Miracles, this is not it. Instead I recommend you Google Marianne Williamson. If you are looking for a practical system to improve your pricing, then continue. There is a lot to cover.

"I think probably the most important thing is having good fundamentals."
- Gordon Moore

CHAPTER 2 - YOUR PRICING BELIEF SYSTEM

In conversations with technology services managers, one of the most frequent questions I get is : "What's the difference between cost based, market based and value based pricing, and why does it matter?" As a career pricer, my initial reaction was that the answer is so fundamental it does not merit a thoughtful response. But as the question kept coming up, it became clear that this fundamental question needed to be answered. Cost based, market based and value based pricing are a company's pricing belief system, and part of the culture. And as in every other human endeavor, belief precedes achievement.

Common TS Pricing Belief Systems

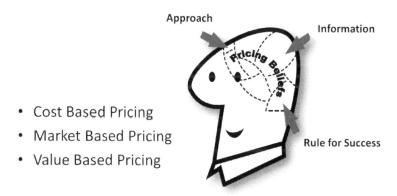

Approach

Information

Pricing Beliefs

- Cost Based Pricing
- Market Based Pricing
- Value Based Pricing

Rule for Success

A company's pricing belief system is a combination of three things: 1) the approach staff generally uses in solving pricing problems, 2) the information the staff uses to inform decisions, and 3) the rules it uses to define success. If your firm practices cost based pricing, your primary information source is internal financial information, your approach is to calculate your costs and add a margin on top, and the rule for success is to hit your target margin. If you are a market based pricer, your primary information needs are prices and perceived value of competitive offerings. Your approach is to evaluate competitive alternatives and to set your price to be "competitive". Your rule for success is to "match the market" while keeping your costs in line. If your organization practices value based pricing, the essential information needed is an estimate of the economic value delivered by your offering relative to the next best alternative. The approach is to set a price that captures a fair share of value delivered given the unique attributes of your offering, the competition and the business impact you have. The rule for success is to set a price that optimizes long term profitability – not revenues.

A company's pricing belief system is the way a firm thinks about pricing most of the time. It is the overarching system managers use to understand what the market wants, how to design an offering and price menu that appeals to customers and what price level and structure the company should set. It is this belief system which governs the firm's pricing behavior. This chapter dives deeply into what each system means and the consequences of relying on that system.

To start, I want to share one of the most telling statistics from our RapidAct analysis of the 2011 TSIA Market Rates Study.[6] The study findings are that roughly 45% of embedded PS organizations use cost based pricing, 40% use market based pricing and 15% use value based pricing. Anecdotal evidence suggests a similar distribution more broadly across services. We looked at the correlation between pricing belief system and profitability at 24 embedded PS organizations (software companies)

Pricing Belief System and PS Profitability
2011 TSIA Market Rates Study

Belief System	Average PS Net Income
Cost Based	11%
Market Based	17%
Value Based	35%

Copyright 2013 Timothy Matanovich

On average, cost based pricers had an 11% operating income, market based pricers had a 17% net income, and value based pricers averaged a whopping 35%. The idea I want to drive home is that how a management team thinks

---

[6] TS Pricing RapidAct™ is a customized analysis and reporting service based on the TSIA Market Rates Study. The service helps cost based pricers make the move to market based pricing.

about pricing has economic consequences. High profit PS organizations predominantly employ market based or value based pricing systems, a clear contrast with less profitable organizations.

Of course many factors contribute to business profitability, but price is without question one of the principal drivers. Based on recent TSIA benchmarking data, a 1% improvement in price translates into an average 8% improvement in PS operating margin.

THE VALUE-PRICE SURFBOARD

To explain the different pricing systems, I will use the Value & Pricing Surfboard, adapted from work by Dr. Irv Gross at the Institute for Study of Business Markets (ISBM) at Penn State.[7] Throughout the book we will revisit the Surfboard to illustrate the impact of pricing practices.

Let's start with Value. The length of the Surfboard is the total Value Delivered by the firm's service offering. You may not be a value based pricer, but the reason customer's choose your offering is that the value they receive is greater than the price in their minds. That said, it is never possible to communicate all the value your offering creates. Your service offering may impact the customer's business in 22,000 ways, but any experienced sales person will tell you the customer only cares about 3-5 things. So a certain percentage of the total Value Created is Value Lost. The remainder is the Value Acknowledged by the customer.

---

[7] Dr. Gross initially called this the "salami". My high tech friends suggested a surfboard would be more appropriate for high tech. ISBM is the leading global academic think tank dedicated to B2B marketing. www.isbm.com

The Value-Price Surfboard

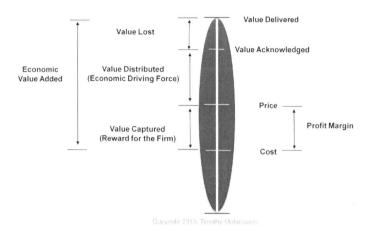

At best the customer will pay a Price equal to the Acknowledged Value of a service. At worst (in most cases) we will sell a service at its Cost. So the widest possible range of prices we could charge for an offering is the range between our Cost and the customer's Acknowledged Value. Perhaps the best way to think about Price is that it is the tool a firm uses to decide how much of the value created is shared with customers and how much it keeps for itself.[8] The value shared is the Value Distributed, and is the Economic Driving Force for the purchase. If there is no gap between the Price and the Acknowledged Value, there is no reason for the customer to buy. The value the firm keeps is the Value Captured, the Reward for the Firm's efforts in creating the value. If there is no gap between the Price and our Cost, there is no reason for the firm to sell.

---

[8] Economic Value Added (EVA) is a term economists use to describe the total value created by a firm.

This idea that price drives behavior is at the heart of good pricing practice. We all know in our bones that price drives customer behavior. It's why we get that lump in our throat when we quote a price. Yet think about how we often set price. "Our costs have gone up by 3% so we should raise our prices by the same amount." We know in our bones that price drives behavior, but we often close our eyes and hope for the best because we lack the tools and practices to think coherently about how that happens. That's what this book is about.

So let's use the Surfboard to look at the three pricing systems.

COST BASED PRICING

The most common pricing model used in technology services is cost based pricing, so let's start there. When cost based pricing is used, firms develop a service offering, calculate the costs of delivery and then think about what price to charge to achieve a margin target. The pricing mantra is *make your margin*.

Cost Based Pricing

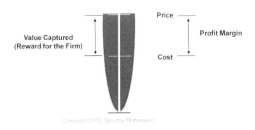

The first thing you notice looking at the Value-Price Surfboard is that you only have half of a Surfboard. Indeed, the primary reasons firms employ cost based pricing is that it is easy to use and it is the lowest cost pricing system. You can go into any surf shop in Monterey and purchase half a surfboard for cheap. In my shopping, one surfer said "You gotta go with the flow man, but that one might be a bummer." Let's see what he means.

Cost based pricing makes intuitive sense. If you understand your costs, and you price higher, you are basically doing the right thing. Of course, during roughly 7,500 years of human civilization the idea that the world was flat, and behaving as if it was, was considered the right thing. But then a guy named Chris challenged the accepted norm and literally changed the world.

You will recall from Marketing 101 in business school that price is one of the four Ps of the marketing mix along with Product, Place and Promotion. Diving a little deeper into marketing, any marketing strategist worth their salt will tell you that the three key elements of marketing strategy are segment targeting, offering design and price. Hence, the primary problem with cost based pricing is obvious: there is no

> *Any marketing strategist worth their salt will tell you that the three elements of marketing strategy are segment targeting, offering design and price. Hence, the primary problem of cost based pricing is obvious: There is no connection whatsoever to what customers are willing to pay. For this reason the words "pricing strategy" and "cost based pricing" cannot be used in the same sentence. Cost based pricing is not strategic.*

connection whatsoever to what customers are willing to pay. The needs of the market are ignored. Where your marketing strategy should be on three legs, you have it teetering on two with cost based pricing.

For this reason, the terms "pricing strategy" and "cost based pricing" cannot be used in the same sentence. Cost based pricing is not strategic. Strategy, by definition, occurs when firms compete for a customer.[9] Here the customer is excluded. Instead, cost based pricing is an expedient response when you must choose a price and no other means is available. If simplicity and low cost are your primary considerations, then cost based pricing can't be beat.

There are some tradeoffs, however, you should be aware of if you rely on cost based pricing. As I said, there is no connection between your costs and what the customer is willing to pay. Anyone reading this who has paid full price for a cell phone, or is willing to pay full price for a cell phone, raise your hand. I don't know the statistics, but I would be willing to bet that fewer than 1% of all cell phones sold to consumers in the US are sold at full price.[10] Here's another one. Any consultant out there who has used cost based pricing, only to have a customer throw it back in your face, raise your hand. I bet 99% of us in professional services have learned that lesson the hard way. Cost based pricing has the potential for seriously getting in the way of sales and marketing.

From these examples, it may sound like the disconnect with the market is an occasional occurrence, more of an annoyance than a day to day issue for

---

[9] Kenichi Ohmae, The Mind of the Strategist, 1972

[10] This is purely a US example. In some global markets, consumers routinely pay full price for cell phones.

technology services. So we need to think about it from a sales perspective to understand how cost based pricing gets in the way of sales day in and day out. When sales is presented with a cost based pricing, it has no connection to the world they live in. They are given a price with no justification for the customer other than this is what it costs us to deliver. Sales in turn hears from customers that prices are too high, and have no defense. Since nature abhors a vacuum, and being a creative bunch, they develop their own pricing system: "customer based pricing" where the mantra is *make the sale*. If customers say our prices are too high, they must be too high, and getting in the way of making sales. It rarely occurs to them that customers may be less than truthful. So sales takes the next logical step. If our pricing is justified based on our costs, then our costs are too high, getting in the way of sales. So sales pushes back on price. You would do the same thing if you were walking in their shoes.

The owner of pricing, often a Director of Finance, in an effort to make his margin, puts controls in place to hold against the pressure. Being the creative bunch they are, sales proactively searches for ways around the controls. Again, not malicious intent, just enlightened self interest. If finance won't give on price, they go to service product managers with dire warnings that the sale will be lost without a price concession. If product managers don't give in, they pressure their sales managers for concessions. In some cases, sales will refuse to take the service offer to the customer without discounting. Sales will give away products and services to close the sale. I have seen discretionary discounting over 40% because sales cannot justify the service price to the customer and controls don't work. Ultimately the Director of Finance becomes labeled as the "VP of No" for standing in the way of sales for no good reason. Raise your hand if you employ cost based pricing and this doesn't sound all too familiar.

Truth is sales may have a point. Let's say you've had a bad year, attach rates are low and service revenues are down. Since costs are now spread over a smaller number of service agreements, costs per agreement go up. Cost based pricing says you should raise your prices to hit your margin targets. So you announce a price rise for sales. Does this make any sense? And the perversion can become worse. Let's say you have a low cost service and a high cost service that each would solve a customer problem equally well. You would rather sell the high cost service because it means higher margin. Sales would rather sell the higher cost services at a discount because it means a larger commission. What does this do to your competitiveness?

And what are costs anyway? Anybody who has had the privilege of diving deeply into understanding costs knows it is no picnic. What is the cost of a technical architect at 25% utilization? At 90% utilization? If we use the service team in Pakistan to take customer service calls and the cost is $1.50 cents per call, the cost is $9.00 for the European call center, and $6.50 for the US call center. What cost should we use for pricing? We could take the average? If we do, how do we account for variances in language and skills and customer requirements? How should we handle overhead costs?

Or what about investments to improve productivity? One PS executive confided that within the next 12 months he will be able to increase the speed and productivity of his implementation team by 50%. With cost based pricing, he has no opportunity to capture a share of the value of that improvement. His costs go down so his prices go down. He creates greater value for customers but can't capture it.

It's not that costs should play no role in pricing. Understanding costs and cost behavior is essential to achieving good margins through good pricing. It's just

42

that cost based pricing is fraught with problems. Despite its prevalence, cost based pricing for technology services is at best a short term solution. Technology services organizations should move away from cost based pricing as quickly as they can.

MARKET BASED PRICING

The second most prevalent pricing belief system employed by TS organizations is Market Based Pricing. In the evolution of pricing capability, this is an important step. It is a step toward a strategic view of pricing where competitor behavior and the role of pricing in creating competitive advantage are considered in decision making. Pricing moves from a being a financial tactic to a strategic decision.

Market Based Pricing

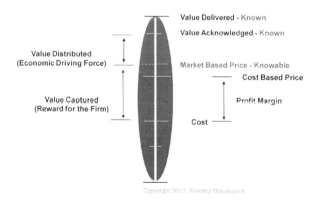

Market based pricing postulates that there is an acknowledged value for the service we are offering, and based on that value there is a "market price". If we can determine what that is, we can price our offering to be "competitive". In many cases, though not all, employing market based pricing results in an offering price that is higher than the cost based price, so we have referenced it as the Market Based Price in the Surfboard.

To understand the kinds of situations where market based pricing works well, let's talk pork bellies. Yes, pork bellies. You can go to the Chicago Mercantile Exchange this very second and get the current price for pork bellies - $81.725. I have no idea what that means, but there it is, the market price. For many commodity products you can find a market price. So market based pricing works best when there is little variance in the quality of competing offerings.

The key to successfully employing market based pricing in services is to understand its primary weakness and compensate for it. That weakness becomes abundantly evident by looking at the following chart of PS List Rates for six job descriptions at software companies selling into Canada.

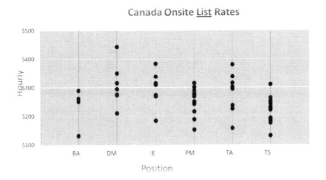

What is the "market rate" for a delivery manager (DM)? The range is roughly $210 per hour from the lowest price company to $450 per hour for the highest price company. Should you take the average at $325 per hour? Should you price in the top quartile or the bottom quartile? How do you know? The answer is important because a 1% variance in PS price is on average an 8% variance in profit, and the potential range here is enormous.

The primary challenge you run into when employing market based pricing in services is that the "market price" in many cases is an illusion. Rather what you have is individual companies with varying strategic intent serving unique segments of customers with offerings that are apples and oranges. The cases where the market price may not be an illusion is in mature, commodity markets where competing offerings are simple and virtually identical. In these cases prices migrate to a relatively narrow band, at a low level relative to costs. Of course, by the time a market is that mature, you really don't care what the market price is. You are either a remaining low cost supplier, you have moved on to greener pastures (cleaner pig pens?), or you are a new entrant with a new business model that can operate at an even lower price point than the incumbents.[11]

The key to success in using market based pricing is in dismissing the notion that there is a competitive market price that we should strive to be at. Instead to

---

[11] If you still need convincing that market price is an illusion, consider the euphemism "like two peas in a pod", indicating a high degree of similarity. Now go to your local grocery store, and go to the canned peas section. How many brands are there, at how many prices? Are any the same? To really stretch your mind, look at the brands of frozen peas as well. Also consider fresh peas. What is the market price?

we should use competing offerings to triangulate on a price that represents fair compensation for the value delivered. In other words, the key to effective market based pricing is the quality of the price planning process and the information you have driving the process. In a high quality market based pricing process, three questions are answered.

1. What is the customer's competitive frame of reference? This is the set of competitors you routinely face, against which you compete for business.

2. What are our strengths and weaknesses relative to competing offerings? Presumably, when customers choose your services, they have other options, even if that means doing it themselves. It is important to understand how your offering stacks up on key attributes that drive value.

3. What are our competitor's prices? Offerings vary by competitor and so do prices. If you are employing market based pricing, good pricing intelligence is important.

In other words, market based pricing is most effective when it begins to lean toward value based pricing. Compared with cost based pricing, market based pricing is a major step in the right direction. By comparing your services with those of the competition, you can provide sales with general guidance on the factors that make your offering strong and why the price is justified.

VALUE BASED PRICING

If the mantra of cost based pricing is to *Make Your Margin*, and the mantra of market based pricing is to *Match the Market*, then the mantra of value based pricing is *Price for Profitable Growth*. In other words, we are not just going to do what is necessary to make a profit. We are not going to shoot for some imaginary target in hopes of making a profit. We are going to have our price be an integral part of our marketing strategy to create competitive advantage and drive profitable growth. That's value based pricing.

To clarify this point, let's turn again to our old friend, the Value - Price Surfboard.

Value Based Pricing

Recall the underlying assumption of market based pricing. There is a market price that we should strive to achieve. By contrast, value based pricing assumes value and price are malleable. By focusing on better understanding our customers and services innovation, we can drive Value Delivered higher. Through our marketing and sales efforts we can drive Acknowledged Value higher. By driving Delivered and Acknowledged Value higher, and better understanding business impact, we can capture a higher Value Based Price.

Here's an example. A company wanted to introduce a new offering that would permit health insurers to better manage the health of their Medicare patients. Since people over 65 account for over half of all healthcare expenditures, the potential value to customers was sizable. Having said that, product and sales managers thought the service should sell for roughly $200,000 per year, because that was near the price of similar offering with similar benefits targeting the general population. Our in-house value analysis suggested that the price level should be roughly $800K. With that wide discrepancy, we decided to research potential customers. That research revealed that prospective customers would be willing to pay $1.6M, twice as high as we thought. When we shared this with the business unit heads, they figured for sure we were smoking something. The offering would never sell for that. After repeated meetings including all sorts of colorful language, we decided on $600K, 3X the original proposed price with an incentive for early adopter customers. The service offering went on to successfully launch and ultimately sell at the target price. In other words, we would have given up at least 2/3 of the revenues on each sale had we not done the value based pricing work. Our experience is that in many cases the value price will be a multiple of the price you will have if you don't do your homework.

When you bring a new service like this to market, how much is it worth to customers? The answer is the service is worth nothing until you tell them how much it is worth. In the case above, if we had gone to market at $200K, the service would have been worth $200k. Since we went to market at $600K, the service was worth $600K. Of course, customers will consider alternatives. But if we have done our homework and know what those alternatives are, we are in a position to define value for the marketplace. This is the true power of value based pricing.

Here's another example. Working part time for five years, and testing it in his own practice, a physician developed a systematic approach for improving efficiency and reducing costs in the typical doctor's office. He assembled the details of his system in a book. Actually, it is more a practice operating manual. The doctor sought our help in pricing. The question he asked when we met was: "What price should I charge for my book?" He reported that books like this at medical conferences sold for $400 to $2,000.

As we talked about his work, we discovered that based on a statistical analysis of typical costs, his own experience and that of close friends, he estimated a cost reduction of 40%. For a medical office generating $1M a year in revenues, annual savings could top $250K. More, with continuing pressure from insurers and government on the top line, cost savings mean continuing practice profitability. In other words, the value of his system was over 100 times the highest price he was considering. When we asked him why he did this work, he replied he wanted to improve the lives of other physicians. When we asked him how likely that would happen if he simply sold a book, he responded that few if any would actually implement his system. At that point his vision of the offering changed. He now saw it as a system to be sold for $20,000 or more that included a guided implementation over 6 months and a performance guarantee.

This is the magic of value based pricing. When you start by asking about value, new opportunities open up that would otherwise not be considered. This suddenly gives you pricing power you didn't know you had. Focus on value and pricing, in turn, tells you what the offering should be. That's what we mean when we say that value and price are malleable.

Now because price and value float together, price is out of the way of sales. In fact, value based pricing has been correlated with both customer satisfaction and employee satisfaction.[12] Everybody benefits from a clear understanding of the connection between value and price, i.e. when company profitability and customer profitability are connected.

Value Based Pricing Connects Profitability through the Value Chain

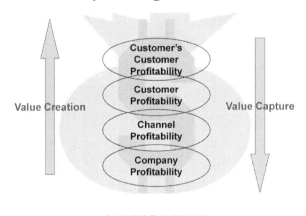

Copyright 2013, Timothy Matanovich

So value by definition is monetized. This is a key differentiator of value based pricing from market based pricing. It is that the firm makes a decided effort to understand the financial impact it makes on the customer's business in dollars and cents terms. This is a clear break from typical market based pricing where the conception of value is based on rating and weighting relative perceived service quality and price. The operative questions for technology services are

---

[12] Gerald Smith, Boston University

1. What is the impact of services on the customer's business?
2. How is that additive to product value?
3. What is unique about our services that meaningfully differentiates us from the competition?
4. How should we capture the value of those services?
5. What might our services sell for if we could better understand value delivered?
6. What is the services value proposition?
7. How does the value prop and value capture change depending on the buying situation or the buyer?

To be clear, it's not that value based pricing leads to value estimated with the accuracy of accounting. Rather, I want to know if I am impacting my customer's business and by roughly how much. Then, if I have 3 potential service investment opportunities, I can choose based on the greatest impact on the customer's business, offering me the highest rewards. Based on that impact, what price can I charge?

Value based pricing goes for the jugular. This is not mamby pamby marketing mumbo jumbo. This is: How much money can I make for my customer? How can I convincingly demonstrate that so they acknowledge the value? How much is a fair share for me to keep? How do I structure the deal to force the customer to pay for value delivered?

Though it takes a fair amount of effort to get to a value based price, in the end the result is simplicity in execution. This is the third key advantage of value based pricing. It is easier for sales and customers. Value based pricing facilitates the development of well defined service offerings and prices that make sense to sales people and the customers they serve. Value understanding is used to tailor communication programs, training programs and negotiation strategies. Value is a basis for triaging price buyers and value buyers, so both can be well served.

You are What You Eat

Not 10 minutes ago I was having a conversation with a group of women who are all losing weight. We talked about how often we go to the gym, what kinds of workouts we do, and our progress and shortcomings. In the end, we had one conclusion – diet is 80% of the solution. No matter how many times a week you go to the gym, if you keep putting too much stuff down your gullet, you are still going to be "big boned".

With cost based pricing, the information is free. You can have all you want and don't have to pay a dime. With market and value based pricing, however, you need to invest in information – market, competitor and value information. You need to add protein to your diet. You need to capture information from your customers using market research techniques. You need to capture competitive information using a third party. The information from your sales organization is biased, plain and simple.

In the last couple of years I have worked with two PS organizations whose sales people were absolutely convinced that their rates were too high. Using TSIA's Market Rates Study we benchmarked their rates against peers. In both cases their rates were the absolute lowest among over 20 peers. I am not saying that they were low or in the bottom quartile. Both companies shared the distinction of being at the absolute bottom of the pile. Since I worked on these two projects at different times, both can share this distinction.

It is the customer's job and in their best interest to tell suppliers that their prices are too high. Your job is to invest in information that disproves what your customers are saying. It's not personal, it's business. We showed the price benchmarking information to sales and raised rates. As of this writing, neither company is worse for the change.

Fortunately, the cost of the information required for market or value based pricing does not have to be high. I just finished working on a proposal for competitor research. Total investment was $14,000. What fraction is that of your latest service sale? How much might an objective view of competitor prices make in your price capture?

A second tradeoff in the shift to both strategic approaches to pricing is the need for new skills. Cost based pricing requires financial skills. Market based pricing requires marketing skills since the key to success is to understand how competing offerings and prices stack up in the marketplace. Value based pricing requires something else – perhaps entrepreneurial skills. The value pricer pushes the envelope, probing for higher profitability. This requires strategic marketing skills, financial skills and sales skills.

"Don't be fooled by the many books on complexity or by the many complex and arcane algorithms you find in this book or elsewhere. Although there are no textbooks on simplicity, simple systems work and complex don't."

- Jim Gray

CHAPTER 3 - THE PROFITABLE TECHNOLOGY SERVICES PRICING (PTSP) SYSTEM

A friend of mine was hired to be the Vice President of Pricing Strategy and was thrilled at the prospect. Unfortunately, he found that his well crafted pricing strategies were discounted away in execution. He might have anticipated this, but there was no effective pricing information system that provided feedback. Building a tracking system helped, but it was actually the pricing process that lacked good controls. Better controls helped, but sales incentives were encouraging the discounting. Better incentives helped, but the sales structure kept the best sales people from working on the best opportunities.

Need I say more? Effective pricing is a system. It works best when the elements of that system work together well. You will be happy to learn, Three chapters into this book, that my goal is not to boil the ocean. (Actually humanity is doing a good enough job of that with or without my help.) But if we are going to manage pricing well, we need a 50,000 foot view. We need to be able to see the big pieces of the pricing puzzle. For those of you who know me and my love of physics, cosmology, space travel and science fiction, it should be no surprise that my vision of the system is *"The Pricing Starship"*.

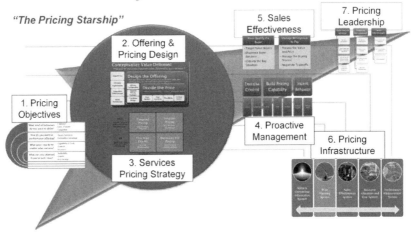

Profitable Technology Services Pricing™
System Overview

Copyright 2013. Timothy Matanovich

Come on. You have hung in this far, honest it really makes sense. And if a few metaphors are stretched, well that's the price of making this interesting enough to actually read.

PRICING OBJECTIVES – CREATING

THRUST

On May 25, 1961 President John Kennedy announced the audacious goal of sending an American safely to the moon before the end of the decade. Only the Panama Canal project in peacetime and the Manhattan Project in wartime compare to the enormous expenditures and effort required to make their respective visions a reality.

Why did the President establish this ambitious and costly enterprise? The answer is that it elevated American prestige during the cold war with the Soviet Union. This was a very visible demonstration of America's strategic technological supremacy.

In the Pricing Starship, the metaphor is thrust. Stage 1 is Pricing Objectives. Objectives provide thrust. If you are engaged in any change management initiative, one of your first activities is to make sure the results of the endeavor will be worthwhile. Change is not easy, so the journey has to be worth the effort.

The good news with pricing is that financial results are often easy to demonstrate. Pricing improvements are percentages of revenues. So if you have a $100M service organization and you improve pricing by 1%, that's a million bucks. And 1% is usually not that hard to find. In many cases the improvements can be a lot more.

Beyond finance, as mentioned earlier, price is a pillar of good marketing and good marketing strategy with implications for targeting and offering design. Pricing drives sales behavior and customer behavior. And pricing sets the stage for sales success.

OFFERING & PRICING DESIGN - THE ENGINE ROOM

As Commander Montgomery Scott on the Starship Enterprise would tell you, the heart of any ship is the engine room. The engine of good pricing is Offering & Pricing Design, stage 2.

Offering & pricing design starts with having an offering that is targeted to meet the needs of a profitable group of customers and is designed to favorably impact the customer's business model. Services offerings are then configured in a way that enables sales directors to sell value when customers want to buy value, and to offer lower prices for configurations that deliver less value. Finally price levels are set to capture a fair share of value created relative to the customer's other options. These three components, value, offering and price comprise the Offering & Pricing Design. Good design drives good behavior from customers and channels.

SERVICES PRICING STRATEGY – THE NAVIGATION SYSTEM

Services pricing strategy, the navigation system, is stage 3 of the PTSP system and aligns pricing objectives with business objectives. This is where technology services pricing is demonstrably unique because of the interplay between the services and the technology they serve (or vice versa). Services pricing strategy varies along two dimensions – the role of the service from the point of view of the customer, and the type of service from an operational standpoint. Essential services and value added services require fundamentally different pricing strategies. To make it more concrete – Level 2 Support pricing is not a linear extension of Level 1 Support pricing. These two offerings, in fact, require fundamentally different pricing strategies. (Have I piqued your interest?)

From an operations standpoint, the process of developing a pricing strategy varies considerably depending on whether you are in an unstructured environment like professional services, or a structured environment like service agreements. In the unstructured environment, the role of sales in the pricing process is much greater with price discovered during the sales process. The service offering is designed for a single customer. In the structured environment, prices are planned in advance, and offerings are designed for target groups of customers.

In sum, Services Pricing Strategy is the navigation system because it aligns pricing with business goals, drives good behavior and provides the sales organization what it needs to succeed.   Sales directors need good value propositions and flexible offerings, the fundamental tools of pricing.   Sales directors need to be able to justify prices to customers and they need to know why different services are priced differently.   Pricing strategy enables sales success.

PROACTIVE MANAGEMENT – POLICIES & PROCEDURES

If you go to the Paris Air Show, you will see aircraft engines on display from GE Aviation, Pratt & Whitney and Rolls-Royce.   They are remarkable pieces of engineering.   Some are models moving inside glass displays.   Some have cutaway views to showcase noteworthy features.   Some are fired up on stands just for the fun of hearing the engine's roar.   Truth be known, however, they are all useless.   An engine alone, sorry Scotty, is just a hunk of metal.   Even if it is running on a stand, it is at best a science experiment.   To be useful, to accomplish a mission, an engine needs a fuselage and a crew.

In my view, most strategies fail not because they are necessarily bad strategies, but because they are poorly executed.   Frankly, if discounting is high, pricing strategy flies out the number 2 airlock.   Pricing execution is the work of sales and the managers who govern their behavior through policies and procedures. This are stages 4 and 5 in the PTSP system.

Execution effectiveness begins with stage 4, Proactive Management.   That is the process of controlling, developing and incentivizing the organization to do the right things. The goal of proactive management is to make the pricing strategy real in the marketplace. It is to take the power of the pricing strategy engine, and the direction from the navigation system, and transmit it through the sales organization. It includes things like the pricing process, training for sales and recognition for good pricing behavior.

SALES EFFECTIVENESS – THE CREW

Ultimately the responsibility for success of the ship's mission is the crew. These are the working stiffs who make things work. Pricing falls to sales directors who deal one on one with customers. After all, nothing really happens until somebody sells something to somebody else. That is stage 5, Sales Effectiveness. In actuality, from a pricing standpoint, sales must do two things. First they need to price qualify the buyer. In other words, is this buyer really interested in what makes our services unique and are they willing to pay more? Or does this buyer view our services as a commodity, focusing primarily on the nickels and dimes? These are the primary questions sales must answer in the field.

The second thing sales needs to do is manage the buyer's behavior. Every customer wants to buy a galaxy class starship for the price of a shuttlecraft, so sales directors need to present the offering in a way that clearly communicates its value. Then, if they get pushback on price, they need to be able to negotiate value tradeoffs for price concessions.

Proactive management and sales effectiveness combine to form Pricing Execution. This is the place to look for quick wins. If you are looking for a quick way to make a little extra profit, focus on pricing execution. Opportunities for improvement are often easy to spot, straightforward to remedy, and quick to take effect.

Pricing Infrastructure – Information and Communication

One of the great innovations in aircraft instrumentation is the heads up display. The HUD gives the pilot all the essential information he needs about his location, targets, altitude, airspeed, etc., without taking his eyes off the sky.

Pricing infrastructure is stage 6 of the PTSP system. It is the set of systems that provide the players with the pricing information they need, when they need it, for price planning, management or execution. That is information about value, about competition, about costs and about policies.

For companies that pride themselves on developing world class systems, it is noteworthy that the pricing infrastructure in technology services often leaves much to be desired.

Pricing Leadership – The Bridge

One of the great scenes of science fiction film was the arrival of Darth Vader in the first Star Wars film. When he walked onto the scene and hoisted the inept Imperial Storm Trooper off the floor, it was immediately apparent who was in charge.

I was teaching a seminar for the American Marketing Association, and reviewing the financial impact of a change in price. For the typical business, a 1% cut in price results in a 10% decrease in profits. One of the seminar attendees, a VP of Marketing, came up at the break and asked me to walk through the arithmetic one more time. After I did he shook his head. He just got a text from his company's president who had been on the golf course with one of their sizable customers. The president had just agreed to knock several percentage points off the company's price for this customer. The VP said that now he had to go back and "repair the damage". The lesson is that just because a decision is elevated doesn't make it a good decision. Executives need to abide by the company's pricing rules.

Stage 7 of the PTSP system is Pricing Leadership. This is the role of executives. Harking back to the heads up display, executives need timely information on the price performance of the company's offerings – both strategic and tactical information. Then they need to use that information to direct good pricing behavior from their organization.

As a speaker once memorably said: "If you don't like what you see at the bottom of an organization, take a look at what's going on at the top".

"Obstacles are the best friends of architecture."
-   Frank Lloyd Wright

CHAPTER 4 - PRICING OBJECTIVES

Make no mistake, the primary reason to improve price performance is profitability. In 2005 I was interviewing with TriZetto Group for the VP of Pricing Strategy & Value job. During my interview with the President, she said in no uncertain terms "the reason we need you is to improve profitability". At the time, TriZetto was $350M in revenues with uninspiring profitability. We were able to change that in a big way over the next few years. Ultimately, more profitable growth is the end result we are looking for in pricing.

As compared to pure product or pure service environments, technology services are unique in that services are delivered in concert with sophisticated, often high priced, products. At minimum services are necessary for the customer to derive value from the product. In other cases, value is delivered primarily by services solving a customer problem, and products are systems for anchoring service value. Pricing objectives are set in the context of this symbiotic relationship. The figure below illustrates the pricing context and the myriad of constraints imposed by the TS environment.

At the center of the figure are the three central issues we must manage for effective pricing

1.   Manage the Value Exchange
2.   Manage Competitor Dynamics
3.   Manage Resources and Costs

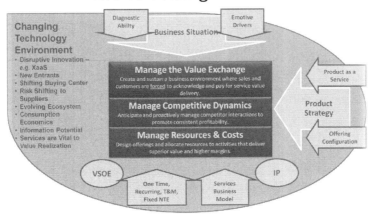

MANAGE THE VALUE EXCHANGE

Effective pricers create and sustain a business environment where both the sales organization and customers are <u>forced</u> to acknowledge and pay for value delivery. That might be easy if more TS managers were named Soprano. As it is, pricers must rely on more socially acceptable means of enforcement. Managing the value exchange begins before the first contact is made with a customer and extends through the final stages of negotiation. The most profitable pricing strategies result when TS:

○ Works with the product organization to choose target customers where they can deliver superior, differentiated value at competitive advantage.

- ○ Understands client business models and client value drivers, particularly related to services
- ○ Constructs service offerings and service options that deliver quantifiable economic impact to target client businesses

Let me use a real training case as an example. I worked with a company that sold software and provided training services to hospital staff. The software was used to manage patient care, and there was a basic training program that provided necessary instruction on how to use the software. As we often find, not all customers are created equal. In this case it was that not all patients are created equal. Perhaps half of the hospital's patients were insured by Medicare. By using the software in a certain way, hospital staff could capture information vital to Medicare reimbursement. In fact, by capturing that information the hospital would qualify for incrementally higher Medicare reimbursement, i.e. the training had a direct impact on the hospital's revenue stream. So instead of adding this information into the basic training program, we created advanced Medicare training. To optimize Medicare reimbursement, the hospital would have to enroll their people in advanced training and pay more.

Note what we did. We needed sufficient understanding of the hospital's business to focus on unique value that would optimize the business impact of our software. We designed a value added training program, above and beyond the basic training, to package that unique value for consumption. That packaging permitted us to force sales and customers to acknowledge and pay for value delivery.

MANAGING COMPETITIVE DYNAMICS

No single action hammers earnings more powerfully than price cuts. For the typical business, a 1% price cut reduces profits by 10%. Competing on price most often is a lose-lose game where not only the competitors are worse off but the customer may be as well. As a customer do you want to do business with an unprofitable supplier? Price wars create unprofitable suppliers. Managing competitive dynamics, therefore, is essential to good pricing. Effective pricers anticipate and proactively manage competitor interactions to promote consistent profitability.

Think of price as the nuclear warhead of the marketing arsenal. No other weapon in that arsenal can be deployed more quickly or with more devastating effect than price. Change your sales strategy or communications strategy or offering mix by 10% and customers may not even notice. Change your price by 10% and not only do customers notice, you may have a revolution on your hands. And that revolution is immediately felt on your bottom line. The lesson is that you only consider deploying a nuclear weapon after carefully considering the strategic consequences.

A price concession in India today haunts you in Canada tomorrow. A deal you cut with Acme Enterprises in Montana today, bites you when Acme is acquired by Roadrunner Corporation in North Carolina and managers want the same deal for all five of their plants. A special price you offered to one customer becomes the topic of a dinner conversation at the American Purchasing Managers Association meeting in Las Vegas. A quick response to an aggressive price move by a competitor in Michigan results in a price war across the Midwest. Each of these cases illustrates the unintended consequences of short term thinking.

Effective pricers get smart about the competition and don't confuse price sensitivity with price competition. All customers can be price sensitive. It may be that changes in their business have reduced the value of what you are offering. It may be that your offering is getting long in the tooth and customers are less willing to pay for it. It may be how you present your offering prompts customers to demand price concessions. Each of these causes price pressure, but none are the fault of the competition.

When competitors are price aggressive, rather than immediately reacting to that aggression, effective pricers consider the long term consequences of their response. If your competitor is strategically and financially stronger than your firm, responding to their aggression may just accelerate your path to financial difficulty. It may be that your competitors' prices are irrelevant because they aren't really competitors for this piece of business. To manage the competition, effective pricers anticipate and proactively manage their competitive arena through:

o   Diagnosing the sources of price pressure to take appropriate action
o   Actively communicating their intentions and capabilities in their market space.
o   Acting consistently with their announced intentions, avoiding opportunistic actions.
o   Evolving their products, services and sources of competitive advantage well in advance of competition.

MANAGING RESOURCES AND COSTS

Effective pricers consistently apply resources to those clients and activities that allow them to deliver superior, differentiated value at competitive advantage.

This is particularly important in TS where the unique capabilities of individuals can make the difference between service success and failure, where utilization can mean the difference between profit and loss and where costs to serve can be complex and variable.

Here the focus on profitability as distinct from revenues comes to the fore. In certain businesses, software for example, variable costs are relatively low. As a result, product revenues and profitability grow hand in hand. Sell more stuff and make more money. In hardware and services businesses, however, variable costs are considerably higher and capacity is limited in the short run. The following chart uses warranty services to illustrate the importance of a focus on profitability distinct from revenues.[13]

Price and the Economics of Services

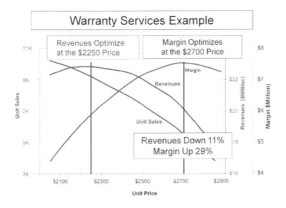

---

[13] This chart is a real technology services case that has been disguised for this use. The relationships were determined using Revenue/Margin Optimization Modeling using customer research as a data source. Source: SDR

You know from your own experience there is a direct connection between the price you charge and the level of demand for extended warranty services. Higher prices less demand; lower prices more demand. In Econ 101, this was described as the demand curve. The red line on the figure above is the demand curve. The green line is the revenue line and largely runs parallel to the demand curve. Sell more units, generate more revenues. So if the goal of the organization is to optimize revenues, that happens at a price of $2,250 annually and a volume of 10,000 warranty units sold, resulting in $22.5M in revenues. At that level, warranty services generate $5.8M in operating profits, represented by the blue line.

Given cost behavior, however, this is far from an optimal margin result. By raising warranty prices to $2,700 per year, this company loses a sizable 45% of its warranty volume, but only 11% of revenues. It also loses the operating costs associated with that volume. The combination of higher price and lower costs increases operating profit to $7.5M, a 29% increase.

My recommendation here is not to recklessly abandon 45% of your customers to optimize profits. Rather it is to evaluate the consequences of decisions so that they may be better informed. When it comes to warranty services, an important performance metric is attach rates. The prevailing industry mindset is that higher attach rates are better than lower attach rates, and so firms work to maximize attach rates. But in this case, optimizing attach rates results in nearly a 1/3 loss of services profit. Is that a fair price to pay? It really depends on your business model and situation. If you are a product provider in the growth phase of the life cycle, maximizing customer satisfaction and attach rates may make sense. Alternatively, if you are a product extender in a more mature market, where product margins are under duress, then optimizing service margins may be central to your financial health. If you are a systems or solution provider, this kind of thinking is vital. The name of the game is optimizing long term services profitability.

Because of cost behavior, optimizing revenues and optimizing profits in the hardware warranty case are not the same. The question remains: Do you want to make more money or sell more stuff? With software and maintenance, for example, when both have very high margins, the economics may be similar so optimization of revenues and margins may be the same point. Let competitive pressures drive down maintenance margins, however, and the solution changes. Many services, for example professional services, have much narrower margins. With PS it is necessary to balance volume requirements to maintain high utilization against higher prices that may drive higher revenues..

In sum, don't make the mistake of assuming that selling more stuff means making more money. And as my friend George reminds me, you can't take market share to the bank. Here are some key points.

- Don't assume that increased volume or higher attach rates are necessarily linked to higher profitability

- Understand the price-volume-cost-profit relationship. Price will drive volume. Use that lever to achieve the profitable growth you want.

> *Because of cost behavior in services, optimizing revenues and optimizing profits may not be the same. The question is: Do you want to make more money or sell more stuff?*

- Don't let a lack of data or precision hold you back. You can get all the cost and cost behavior data you need from a good finance guy over lunch. If it is more complex than the size of a napkin, you are over thinking the problem. If the consequences are really large, then you can afford to get a cost accountant to give you the precision you need.
- Use breakeven analysis to model price elasticity. Higher prices generally translate to lower volume.

REVENUE/MARGIN OPTIMIZATION

In some cases, the analysis is not as simple as presented above. The goal is not to optimize the profitability of the service alone, but to optimize the overall profitability of the service line or a product service combination. Let's use an example to clarify.

A company has three support levels for their products. Let's call them Bronze, Silver and Gold for simplicity. The executive wants to increase support service profitability and wants to know how much he can increase price without turning away too many customers. The implication is that we should increase price across the board to achieve that result.

The problem is tradeoffs. Let's say Bronze customers are about at their limit. They won't pay another cent for support and are happy to share their perspective in colorful terms with anybody who wants to know. Raise prices on bronze and you lose customers big time. On the other hand, Gold customers may be thrilled with the value of the service they are receiving and willing to pay more. Silver service customers might be willing to shift to Gold service if the price were just a little lower. To complicate matters, margins are different for each service level because of unique resources used by each. The profit

71

optimization issue in this case is not the profit of a single service level. The goal is to optimize the profitability of the overall service portfolio, but because of the interactions between service levels the answer is not easy to come by. In pricing parlance, this is the substitution effect. It occurs any time customers trade off one offering for another as a result of a pricing decision. When you change prices across a portfolio of services, you run into the substitution effect.

Now before you throw your hands up in despair, or throw this book against the wall while using the aforementioned colorful language, know that there are ways to sort through this. Working with a group of sales people over the course of a day or two you can actually model this out. Alternatively, and much better, you can get feedback directly from customers and model it. The result is a profit optimization across a portfolio of services that permits you to set prices that actually optimize service line profitability.

Another factor to consider in optimizing margin decisions is the impact of the sale of one service on the demand for another product or service. This is called the complimentary offering effect. This is the justification for loss leaders. If I let you buy a cell phone cheaply, you are more likely to sign up for a two year service agreement. If I sell my equipment into a power plant at a low price, I can sell them high priced sundries, parts and services for decades. Typically the complementary offering effect results in prices for an initial offering that are lower than they might otherwise be.

SERVICES STRATEGY AND PRICING OBJECTIVES

In his book *Crossing the Services Chasm*, Thomas Lah asserts that it is important for services organizations to have a well defined strategy.[14] That strategy is set in relationship to the firm's core technology and its place in the life cycle. So, for example a firm with a software product in a rapid growth market will have a services strategy different than a firm with a product in maturity. Following are the service strategy profiles.

Services Strategy Profiles & Fit with the Technology Life Cycle

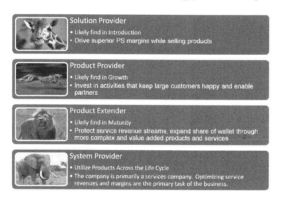

Solution Provider
- Likely find in Introduction
- Drive superior PS margins while selling products

Product Provider
- Likely find in Growth
- Invest in activities that keep large customers happy and enable partners

Product Extender
- Likely find in Maturity
- Protect service revenue streams, expand share of wallet through more complex and value added products and services

System Provider
- Utilize Products Across the Life Cycle
- The company is primarily a services company. Optimizing service revenues and margins are the primary task of the business.

Adapted from *Bridging the Services Chasm* by Thomas Lah,

Copyright 2013, Timothy Matanovich

Pricing objectives also vary by stage in the life cycle, though the relationship is more granular than that of service strategies. For example, a company's core technology may be in the maturity stage of the life cycle and therefore its

---

[14] Thomas Lah, Bridging the Services Chasm: Aligning Services Strategy to Maximize Product Success

services strategy would be a Product Extender. The firm, however, has also matured, likely having a portfolio of products. Some of these products will be in the introduction stage, others in the growth stage and still others in the maturity stage. Pricing is part of product/market strategy. So pricing for products and services in each stage of the life cycle will vary.[15] Here are the fundamentals.

INTRODUCTION STAGE – TECHNOLOGY ENTHUSIASTS AND VISIONARIES

During the introduction stage of the technology life cycle, the firm will encounter two types of buyers – technology enthusiasts and visionaries. Basically neither have much money, but visionaries may be able to access money. In both cases the economic value of the offering is relative to an incumbent solution. That is, when you sell your solution you make your case compared to the customer's current inefficient/ineffective process. Since the product is unproven, services lead with the objective of solving the customer's problem. That means services are priced for value and the product is priced for penetration.

You have two goals during the introduction stage. The first is to define the core offering, i.e. the product and service attributes that solve the customer's problem. The second is to discover and demonstrate substantial and repeatable value delivery. In other words, solving one customer's problem is nice, but finding a solution that solves a high value problem encountered by many potential customers is where the real money is.

---

[15] We are using the terminology here from Geoffrey Moore, Crossing the Chasm: Marketing and Selling Disruptive Products to Mainstream Customers

GROWTH STAGE - PRAGMATISTS

If you have succeeded in finding a high value, repeatable solution then you are in growth mode. More than likely you are beginning to see direct competitors emerge. At this point your value reference shifts from the customer's incumbent process to a competitor's alternative solution. In introduction the question was: How good are you? In growth the question is: How good are you relative to your closest competitor?

Segmentation begins to emerge. Your offering is best suited to some customers and your competitor is better suited to others. This leads to refinement in offering design and pricing. Customers are pragmatists and expect a product that works with little operational disruption. Since the product has "taken off", now the product is priced for value relative to competitive alternatives. Things can change fast as competitors compete to be the last man standing, and prices can fall rapidly. Services take a back seat, priced for penetration. In essence, keep the services out of the way of product sales and let's enjoy the "tornado".

MATURITY STAGE - CONSERVATIVES

Every offering class ultimately reaches maturity. Growth slows and the few remaining competitors are in it for the long haul. At this point prices and market shares stabilize. The pricing objective is to not rock the boat. New customers are conservatives. Keep your costs down and don't compete on price. Since market shares won't change, price competition simply reduces profitability for everybody.

With existing customers, services come to the fore. Firms seek new opportunities to create value for long term customers. These may be product opportunities or service opportunities. The goal is to expand the footprint and utilization. These incremental revenues may become very important to the overall profitability of the firm. As I write this it occurs to me that these stages are not discrete, but blend into one another. Expansion of utilization may begin during the growth stage.

Simultaneously essential service prices may come under pressure and defending them becomes another priority. To a product extender, services and service prices are important issues.

NOTE ON SERVICE PROVIDERS

In each of the above life cycle stages, the services strategy and broad guidelines for service pricing are determined by the role of the product in the mix. During introduction, service pricing is at the forefront. During growth, service pricing takes a back seat. During maturity, service pricing re-emerges.

Not so with service providers, the fourth service strategy profile. These are firms that are service providers first and product providers second. For these firms selling service value is always the priority. Product value is secondary.

BUSINESS SPECIFIC OBJECTIVES

The range of business situations where pricing applies, and where pricing objectives and strategy are required, is quite broad. So we have chosen a handful of situations and described pricing objectives in each.

NEW OFFERING DESIGN

The role of price in new offering design is the classic pricing strategy case with four distinct stages. The question "what price should you charge" is only the beginning.

If you have an offering that has great potential, but is unproven in many ways, you may want to set a Beta price that gets you trial with a select group of customers. At this stage, there may be little cash transacted. Rather the price you demand is information, an important part of which is value delivered. You want to answer questions like

- How does my offering impact the customer's business model?
- What business processes are streamlined or made more effective?
- What is the dollar value of the cost savings or revenue enhancement that we create?
- How does that dollar value scale with the size of business?
- How do the product and service elements contribute to value delivered?
- How do the answers to these questions vary from customer to customer?

Answers to these value questions lay the foundation for setting price level and structure for customers more broadly. The questions also set the stage for identifying value buyers and for forecasting demand and revenues that drive the business model.

Your next level of pricing is for Early Adopters. Here you test your pricing by getting real customers to buy at a price approaching your ultimate final price. Normally a price incentive is required, but the value proposition and offering are fairly well developed. The price is a combination of cash payment plus information plus a risk adjustment that recognizes the inherent risk of the new offering. An important part of the information you need from early adopters is confirmation of value delivered on a broader scale. Here you start building value cases that document how value is delivered and when. Your documentation may lead you to revise your value proposition and pricing for launch into the Early Majority.

Selling to the Early Majority is the final phase of launch pricing. Your offering configuration (products plus services) is determined by your primary target growth markets. Likewise, your price level determines what segments your offering will appeal to and the proportion of customers who will buy. Higher price, fewer customers. Lower price, more customers.

If your offering creates real value for customers in the early majority, competitors will enter. At this point value propositions will diverge as competitors focus on different market segments. The final element of launch pricing is to tailor pricing to different segments, especially defending those segments where the company has competitive advantage and high margins can be maintained.

So the simple question, what price should I charge, translates into beta price, early adopter price, early majority price and competitive price.

MIGRATION STRATEGY

Let's say you are not only introducing a new offering, but phasing out an old one. Here the role of price in driving behavior comes to the forefront. The price you charge for your new offering will determine how quickly customers migrate from the old. If you set a higher price for your new offering, migration will be slower, but profitability of your service portfolio may be enhanced. More, by pricing your new offering higher you will discover which customers truly value your new offering because they will be your first customers at the higher price.

Alternatively, pricing lower will encourage migration. Whichever path you choose, by offering a migration strategy you give customers options. That's a good thing. Customers like options. They usually dislike being dictated to, which is essentially what you are doing when you simply replace one offering with another.

Migration from legacy software licensing to software-as-a-service is a specific case where migration pricing strategy can powerfully drive profitability during the transition. A key piece of the pricing work is to abandon preconceptions and open your eyes to the range of pricing possibilities. Pricing flexibility is often greater than you realize and risks are often lower than you realize.

PRICE SEGMENTATION

Perhaps the single most powerful tool in the pricer's arsenal is price segmentation. The following example from the hotel industry illustrates how price segmentation can work to better serve your customers, give sales clearer direction and make more money for your firm.

Market strategy is the combination of target customer plus offering plus price that creates a win-win relationship between buyer and seller. As a strategist, your price determines the target market you are after. As a strategist you need to answer the question: Are we the Waldorf Astoria or the Hampton Inn? These are two of the ten brands that comprise Hilton Hotels.

Perhaps the single most powerful tool in the pricer's arsenal is price segmentation. Market strategy is the combination of target customer plus offering plus price that creates a win-win relationship between buyer and seller. As a strategist, your price determines the market you are after. As a strategist you need to answer the question: are you the Waldorf Astoria or the Hampton Inn?

The truth is that you actually want a pricing strategy that gets in the way of some sales. Continuing the example, The Waldorf price gets in the way of more sales than the Hampden Inn price, and that's OK. Your strategic pricing decision is to decide what sales you want to get in the way of and which ones you don't and then to communicate that to the sales organization. You want sales chasing the right kinds of deals. Your strategic market segmentation provides vital direction to sales, resulting in higher sales effectiveness and lower sales costs.

Note that once you have made that "price positioning" decision, price competition immediately diminishes. Waldorf competes with the Four Seasons and Ritz Carlton. It competes as a luxury hotel, at a luxury price point. These hotels in no way compete with the Hampton Inn or Courtyard by Marriott. This latter group competes for the day to day business traveler, at a day to day business price point. Each of the ten brands in the Hilton portfolio competes at a different price point.

Now let's say you have decided you are the Hampton Inn, competing with Courtyard across the street. Tactical pricing begins with understanding your business economics. You only have so many rooms, and at full capacity customer service suffers. The Courtyard across the street has the same problem. So your goal is to hit a target range of occupancy where your contribution to overhead is high and customers are well served.

On the revenue side, you need to understand the demand for your hotel rooms. Is it visitors to the IBM facility across the street, visitors to the convention center down the block or visitors to the Six Flags over the hill. The types of buyers determine your offering packages. Obviously, your value proposition for IBM, conventioneers and vacationers are going to be different, with pricing that is tailored to each. Segmentation and targeting remain at the forefront, provides day to day guidance to marketing and sales.

In sum, your price strategy informs your sales people about the kinds of buyers they need to be chasing. Your pricing tactics have created prices that are tailored to the needs of these buyers. Both are built on the foundation of good segmentation and targeting. Good strategic and tactical pricing reduces the level of price competition. Sound pricing, therefore, becomes an aid to sales rather than an impediment, resulting in shorter sales cycles, happier customers and more money for commissions.

PRICE MENU: HAVE YOUR CAKE AND EAT IT TOO

In many B2B pricing situations, especially in services, customers are price inelastic, i.e. they are more sensitive to changes in value than changes in price. As a result, companies find they may be able to raise prices to increase profitability. Doing that, however, may result in losing some lower end customers. One PS organization found that raising prices increased project margins, but overall margins decreased because utilization fell.

This dilemma illustrates the problem of one price fits all, aka monopriceosis.[16] The appropriate pricing strategy here is to design the offering and price menu such that low priced customers get streamlined service offerings and those that want greater value pay a higher price. Of course, there are tricks to the trade. The offerings must be designed with sufficient value differences across options that persuade certain customers to choose the higher priced options. In addition we must erect "fences" to keep buyers separated.

Note this is not the same as giving sales people pricing flexibility to adjust price for individual customers. When you give sales authority for price flexibility, they will use price (discounting) to close deals. As a result, all prices will migrate to a lower level. The strategic pricing approach is to segment customers and craft a price menu that forces value-price tradeoffs, i.e. provides sales people with governance that protects high price business. These rules strengthen sales ability to communicate more powerfully and negotiate more effectively.

---

[16] The term monopriceosis was coined by a professor at a mid Atlantic business school whose name I have forgotten.

STRATEGIC OR EXECUTIONAL OBJECTIVES?

Broadly speaking there are two types of pricing objectives – strategic and executional. Strategic pricing objectives have to do with list prices on your price sheet, and executional pricing objectives have to do with invoice or pocket prices. When faced with a pricing challenge or opportunity, a great question to ask is: Is this a strategic or executional pricing issue? That answer can move you quickly down the road to solution.

Pricing strategy begins with understanding value for customers and how that value differs across customers or groups of customers. Strategy includes list prices and the price structure as it is presented to sales on the price sheet. Strategy has to do with enabling sales with a value prop that works.

Pricing execution begins with sales. Does sales have the incentives and capabilities to do what is asked of them? Are they structured in a way that matches up with customer needs and facilitates good pricing behavior? Then there is price management. Is management providing sales with the communication and negotiation tools they need to be successful? Has management taken the pricing strategy and translated that into policies, processes and controls that work?

PRICING OBJECTIVES - IN SUMMARY

Let's summarize the key principles in setting pricing objectives by listing four questions. Then we will quickly review the answers to each.

1. What sales, channel, customer and competitor behaviors are we trying to drive?

2. How do we want to position our value as it relates to target customer needs and relative to the competition?

3. How have we enabled sales success through targeting, offering configuration and price design?

4. What level of sales do we need in order to achieve optimal utilization and profitability?

DRIVING BEHAVIOR

In some cases, as with implementation costs, you want price to be invisible to the degree possible. You don't want to rock the boat. In other cases you want customers to respond to the price, as in choosing between two service levels. In either case, there is a recognition that price can be a powerful driver of behavior. It drives customer behavior, sales behavior, channel behavior and competitor behavior. In setting prices, therefore, the first question to ask is: What kind of behavior do we want to create? In solving pricing problems, the question is: What behaviors do we want to change?

Keep in mind that pricing behavioral changes can be immediate. Ad agencies will tell you that you need to hit customers on the head with an ad ten times before you have recognition; maybe more for the message to get through. With price it can be once. Show them a price and they respond, period.

Price has an immediate impact with sales, and that impact depends on their incentives. If they are paid on volume or revenues, sales people will rely on discounting to close deals. They will even go so far as to work around controls to get the price they want. Alternatively if they are paid on margin or price achievement, then they will hold price and rely much less on discounting.

POSITIONING

Lincoln, Yugo, Nova, Mustang, Ferrari, Chevy – each of these brands evokes an image of the buyer, a set of attributes in your mind and a price point. Price is a vital element of positioning any offering, including technology services. When you set your price you are deciding who can afford your services and who can't. You are, in shorthand, summarizing your value prop and impact on the customer's business. You are positioning yourself against your primary competition and demonstrating your competitive advantage.

The following graph summarizes the four principles pricing objectives.

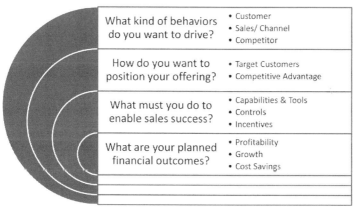

Profitable Technology Services Pricing™
1. Pricing Objectives
What do we want pricing to accomplish?

What kind of behaviors do you want to drive?	• Customer • Sales/ Channel • Competitor
How do you want to position your offering?	• Target Customers • Competitive Advantage
What must you do to enable sales success?	• Capabilities & Tools • Controls • Incentives
What are your planned financial outcomes?	• Profitability • Growth • Cost Savings

Copyright 2013, Timothy Matanovich

ENABLE EXECUTION

If you provide sales with clear value propositions that tie directly to improving the customer's business condition and define those services well, sales will sell them at a fair price. If the value prop isn't clear and services are not well defined, they won't sell services at any price. If you provide sales with an offering that can be configured to individual customers, they will sell to a broader base of customers. If you don't, they won't. If you provide sales with a price menu that facilitates value tradeoffs for price concessions, then you will maintain higher margins. If sales negotiates price, lower margins are likely to result.

FINANCIAL OBJECTIVES

Price is a powerful driver of profitability. Pricing can be used to drive revenues and growth, and to lower costs. Consciously decide what level of growth and profitability you want. Don't assume increased revenues and attach rates necessarily add up to higher profitability.

"Competitive strategy is about being different. It means deliberately choosing a different set of activities to deliver a unique mix of value. . . . If all you're trying to do is be essentially the same as your rivals, then it's unlikely you'll be very successful."

- Michael Porter

CHAPTER 5 – OFFERING & PRICING DESIGN

What is pricing strategy? That question occupied a host of pricing professionals for weeks recently on a popular social networking site. Applying the principle of simplicity for the technology services environment, we define pricing strategy as setting list prices for an offering to achieve business objectives in its target market. Pricing is strategic because it is a powerful driver of customer behavior, can be a key differentiator of the brand and is instrumental to profitable growth.

Pricing strategy also sets up sales success, a role often underappreciated. Pricing strategy is about understanding value delivered and setting a price structure and levels that make sense to sales. It is no revelation that in many cases sales people struggle with services because pricing is complex and difficult to communicate. Weak pricing strategy leads to excessive discounting, longer sales cycles, costly negotiation losses and ultimately low selling prices. Effective pricing strategy results in service pricing that is justifiable to customers, is easy to communicate and has options that force customers to trade off value to secure a lower price so pricing integrity is maintained.

Service pricing integrity is especially important in a global marketplace. Assume for a minute that your pricing practices were totally transparent to all your customers. I know the thought of global transparency may make your heart race. It's OK. Calm down. Cue up that meditation music you have on your iPod. Sip some chamomile tea. Okay? Better now? Then let's proceed.

The first condition of pricing integrity is that the firm is able to justify pricing variances to its customers. For example, one customer gets a lower price because they consume fewer services. Another pays a higher price because of their unique requirements. Price variances are not due to the negotiating strength and discretionary discounting conferred on different customers, but for real differences in value received.

A second condition of pricing integrity is that it exists from one country to the next. So when a Chinese firm purchases an American firm and rationalization occurs, the differences in the China and US prices can be justified.

Pricing Strategy

Copyright 2013 Timothy Matanovich

Pricing strategy is outward facing. It is a statement by the firm about how it wants customers and competitors to respond to its pricing. It is a statement that recognizes that price is arguably the single most powerful communication you have with your customers. In a heartbeat, when you quote your price, you tell the customer the value of your offering and how it stacks up against the competition.

PRICING STRATEGY: MARKET BASED OR VALUE BASED?

In technology services, three pricing models are prevalent: cost based pricing, market based pricing and value based pricing. Of these, only market based pricing and value based pricing are strategic. Cost based pricing ignores the market and is not strategic.

Considering market based pricing and value based pricing, which strategic pricing approach should you use? That depends on your objectives. If you are looking to make the easiest transition from cost based pricing, then market based pricing is your best move. This is especially true if you believe your prices are low relative to peers and you don't believe there is a high degree of price sensitivity with customers. It is important to distinguish here between customer price sensitivity and sales force price sensitivity. The two are not the same. I have seen numerous occasions where sales is highly price sensitive but customers express few concerns.[17]

---

[17] Win-loss analysis, conducted by an independent third party, is an excellent approach for evaluating customer price sensitivity.

On the other hand, if services revenues are strategically important to the firm, or if you are looking to make a strategic investment in services, then value based pricing is your best choice. Market based pricing generally is not as effective as value based pricing in facilitating service based growth opportunities, and therefore not as good at guiding strategic services investments.

The following table expands on our earlier table and highlights key factors in the choice between cost based, market based pricing and value based pricing.

Pricing Belief System
Profitability & Best Use

Belief System	Average PS Net Income*	Best Use in Technology Services
Cost Based	11%	• When you need pricing quickly with little cost and effort • When you serve a homogenous market • Note: CBP is not a strategic approach to pricing
Market Based	17%	• When services revenues are relatively unimportant to the business • When there are many customers and competitors, and differentiation is limited
Value Based	35%	• When service revenues and margins are important to the business • When services are instrumental in differentiating your offering • When your market is comprised of relatively few, large customers

*Source – 2011 TSIA Market Rates Study

In sum, choose market based pricing if services differentiation is not critical for you and you believe your services are roughly equal to competitors. Choose value based pricing if services differentiation is key to your growth and profitability, and customers are price sensitive or competitive intensity is high. Let's try this as a metaphor. Market based pricing will bring you to the dance.

Value based pricing brings you in a gown from Versace. Which you choose is based on your budget and your objectives.

Historically, when technology services have been primarily essential services, market based pricing fit the bill. The approach is fairly easy to implement. In product driven companies, where the bulk of the value created was through products, market pricing for services worked well enough. Even in the years ahead, market based pricing may remain an acceptable standard in many market situations.

Looking ahead, however, as services become a larger part of the value proposition and are used to differentiate the firm alongside products, market pricing falls short. In the future I believe value driven pricing will become central to the financial health of services businesses. Here's why:

1. Market based pricing won't defend maintenance, value based pricing will.
2. Market based pricing won't help you in major accounts, value based pricing will.
3. Market based pricing won't help you price high value services that drive high financial returns for your customers, value based pricing will.
4. Market based pricing won't help you price new to the world value added services, value based pricing will.
5. Market based pricing won't be as useful as value based pricing in managing discounting.
6. Market based pricing won't help you respond strategically to competitive threats as well as a value based pricing approach.

7. Market based pricing won't help you identify low value services that can be trimmed to save money, value based pricing will

Given these advantages, the PTSP system is a value based pricing system.

OFFERING & PRICING DESIGN

The foundation of pricing strategy is offering & pricing design. As described earlier, this is the engine room. This is where pricing power starts. So what are the essential components of design? The following figure illustrates.

Offering & pricing design in the PTSP system, involves three broad activities: conceptualizing value delivered, designing the offering and price and finally deciding the price, in that order. As described in the chapter on pricing belief systems, the great advantage of value based pricing is that value and price are malleable. You can design an offering that is unique, you can produce a marketing campaign that communicates that unique value and you can capture a price that reflects that unique value. This process makes that belief system real.

It's not magic. In fact, learning to think this way can be challenging. But as with any other business process you get better at it the more you practice and ultimately it becomes the cultural norm and a process of continuous improvement. From my vantage point writing this, I can't tell where you are in the journey. My experience tells me that for some of you this is old hat. For others, this is fresh as 12 inches of morning powder on peak 8 at Breckenridge. If you are in the latter group, take heart. This all starts with a team conversation. 80% of what you need to know, you already know, though you may not know you know it. You can find out more through conversations with customers. You just may not have applied it in this way before.

CONCEPTUALIZING VALUE DELIVERED

A long, long time ago a marketing guru named Ted Levitt explained the concept of value very simply. "People don't buy quarter inch drills because they want quarter inch drills. They buy quarter inch drills because they want quarter inch holes."[18] Conceptualizing value delivered is the search for the holes.

---

[18] Theodore Levitt, The Marketing Imagination

VALUE DRIVERS

Reflect for a moment on your own life in the world of business. What consumes your days? For most of us we strive daily to make our business better. We are searching for new customers. We are developing new products. We are improving processes. We are launching new initiatives. We are managing budgets. What we don't do is spend our days thinking about our suppliers' products and services. If we do think about them, it is in the context of our objectives. For example, as a pricing manager if I am thinking about hiring a pricing researcher, it is in the context of a new product launch or optimizing profitability of that launch.

Value drivers are the handful of priorities a business has for cost management or revenue/margin increase. <u>Customer value drivers are independent of your offerings</u>. They are the customer's business priorities. In the oil and gas business, for example, a critical issue is regularity of supply. Anything that gets in the way of supply, impedes production, harming revenues. If product can't be refined and transported, it can't be sold. In the chemical business, transportation safety is a value driver. Chemical firms place a high value on anything that can assure their products move without incident.

> *One of the great advantages of this process is that it forces you to look at the world from the point of view of your customer*

The end objective is to tie your service offerings to the critical managerial priorities of your customers: what they value rather than what they don't. One of the great advantages of this process is that it forces you to look at the world from the point of view of your customer, independent of your offerings. How refreshing will it be for your customer when you ultimately sit down with her and have a conversation about her business priorities?

CUSTOMER SEGMENTATION

Every single customer receives different value from the firm's offerings. Some customers are more willing to pay for value than others. Some customers are simply more valuable to the firm than others. Pricing strategy, therefore, like overall business and marketing strategy, begins with an understanding of segmentation.

From a services pricing perspective, the goal of segmentation is to identify groups of customers with common service needs in order that a service mix and price menu can be tailored to them. If the firm has a professional services practice and employs value based pricing, then the service offering may be configured for a segment of one – this customer. If you are a hardware company, designing service agreements, then identifying groups of customers with common needs is instrumental to developing a service plan and a pricing menu that makes sense for those customers.

Good segmentation is particularly important in services because in many cases, the ability to customize the product for specific applications is constrained. As a result, services are vital to tailoring the product to the needs of individual customers.

Segmentation for pricing is often different than the segmentation schemes the firm is using for other purposes. Because the conceptualization of value is central to pricing strategy, we strongly advocate a value driven approach to segmentation, i.e. a segmentation approach that directly links to the customer's value drivers. The figure below illustrates one firm's approach to value driven segmentation.

Value Driven Segmentation

		High Volume Producers		Solution Providers	
Downtime Economic Impact	High	• Rapid Response • JIT Inventory • Production Efficiency	• Rapid Response • JIT Inventory • Production Efficiency • Environmental Sensitivity	• Rapid Response • JIT Inventory • Rapid NPD Process • Responsiveness to Customer Technical Needs • Speed to Market	• Rapid Response • JIT Inventory • Rapid NPD Process • Responsiveness to Customer Technical Needs • Speed to Market
	Low	• Internal Efficiencies (May have similar value drivers as other segments, but prefer in-house capabilities)	• N/A	• Responsiveness to Customer Technical Needs	• Rapid NPD Process • Responsiveness to Customer Technical Needs • Environmental sensitivity
		High	Low	High	Low
		Internal Technical Support Capabilities			

Instead of looking at customers by firmographic characteristics, we conceptualize a framework that looks at commonalities in their business models. In this example, some customers are high volume producers, others are solution providers. In the heavy duty trucking market, for example, Sterling produces a good truck for a broad base of customers where low prices are essential to market success. Peterbilt produces trucks for high stress, specialized applications that sell at higher prices. On their web site, they offer to "put you in the driver's seat and build a truck around it". So if your services excel in helping your customers tailor solutions and shorten time to market then you have a good fit with solution providers like Pete. If your services excel at helping your customers increase efficiency in operations, then you might fit better with high volume producers like Sterling. Maybe you deliver both. The point is that conceptualizing segmentation based on key elements of the customer's business model provides insight into how customers choose between competitors and what services they value most.

> *Serving 22 verticals with unique needs is a nightmare. Serving 5 value segments with common needs across verticals simplifies life considerabley*

Continuing with the example, downtime has a significant financial impact on some customers, but not on others. Finally, some customers need a high degree of technical support, others are largely self sufficient. On this latter point, it is obvious that service offerings to customers than have a high need for tech support will be different than those that are largely self sufficient.

In sum, the company has conceptualized a three dimensional value driven segmentation framework. This segmentation sets the stage for a services mix that delivers different value propositions to different customers in a way that makes sense to them and makes business sense for the firm. Serving 22 verticals with unique needs is a nightmare. Serving 5 value segments with common needs across verticals simplifies life considerably. This is the foundation for creating a price menu that is both easy to use and forces customers to trade off value for lower prices. Downstream, it is the foundation for effective execution because it provides sales with clear guidance about which service offerings are the best fit for which customers.

Once value driven segmentation has been conceptualized, we can then transition back to more traditional firmographics to test the validity of the segmentation scheme, to assess its usefulness for targeting and to evaluate the economics of the pricing decisions. Continuing with this example, a pricer would ask: Which existing or prospective customers fall into each segment? This would validate the scheme. Note the example includes an "N/A" in one cell. Evidently there are no customers with a business model that is a high volume producer, has a low economic impact from downtime and has low internal technical support capabilities.

Once we validate that customers exist across segments, we may want to do some demand planning. For example, all things being equal, a field service agreement at a price of $500K per year will have fewer customers than a service agreement priced at $100K per year. Think about the demand curve you learned about in Econ 101. So we might look across segments and hypothesize how much customers in each segment might be willing to pay based on value received. Price paid times number of customers in each segment will give us a revenue picture of the services portfolio. Services required by segment, then, gives us our costs, so value based segmentation underlies the business economics of the services portfolio.

If you find that customers flock to one service offering, for example your lowest priced offering, then a look at segmentation might be a good place to begin the diagnostic. Customers flock to single offerings because the value props of other offerings are not compelling. They are often not compelling because they don't adequately meet the needs of a unique segment of customers.

COMPETITIVE DIFFERENTIATION

The first element of conceptualizing value is determining value drivers. The second is competitive differentiation. As the segmentation analysis abundantly illustrates, service needs of business customers are value based. What is value? Value is impact on the customer's business model, i.e. what the business does and how it makes money doing those things[19]. The better your services are at impacting the customer's business model, helping them lower their costs or increasing revenues and margins, the greater the pricing power you have with those services. Competitive differentiation is the degree to which your impact on the customer's business model is different from that of competitive alternatives. Compeittive differentiation in services means that there are service based reasons why customers choose to do business with you.

Services differentiation is an important element of total offering differentiation because no matter how flexibly your product can be configured, it is service that leverages that product to impact each individual customer's business model. This is IBM's bet – service differentiation trumps product differentiation most of the time.

As we think about differentiation and competition, it is important to frame the competitive set from a services standpoint. In technology services, I think there are three ways to frame the competitive set in establishing your differentiation, and each fits with a given buy situation.

1. Whole Offering Differentiation
    - If you are a product company and the service sale is at the time of the product sale, then the customer is looking at the

---

[19] Peter Weill, et al, Do some business models perform better than others? A study of the 1000 largest US firms. MIT/Sloan

whole offering, product plus service combined. Framing the competition, the relevant competitive alternatives are your whole offering vs. theirs.

2. Service Offering Differentiation

- If you are in a service only sales situation, and external competitors are viable alternatives for your customer, then the customer is considering your services vs. the services of your competitor. Framing the competition in this case is your service offering vs. that of other service providers.

3. Service Level Differentiation

- If you are in a service only sales situation, and external competitors are not viable alternatives for your customer, then the only choice a customer has is between levels of your service, including the option of not choosing your service. Framing the competition here is your service level 1 vs. service level 2.

In technology services I have seen companies incorrectly frame the competitive set in a way that tends to over emphasize competitive intensity. For example, confusing 2) service offering competition with 3) service level competition would tend to increase the sense of competitive intensity.

In assessing competitive differentiation, it is not only important to understand service differentiation but also how those services impact the customer's business. For example, the quality of your technical services may permit your customer to avoid the cost of hiring several technical specialists. In this case, if the customer chose your competitor they would have to hire several people to achieve a comparable level of overall performance. This differentiation is vital to making the case with your customer for why they should pay your price.

Needless to say, good pricing strategy relies on good information about competitors. Essentially we need to know two things about the competition: their prices and how those prices vary based on services delivered. So where do you get the information? The place to start is with your sales and support organizations, they are your eyes and ears in the field. Put a group together in a room for a day and they will provide you with their shared vision of the competition. That exercise will give you 80% of what you need to know. Marketing organizations often have someone assigned to competitive intelligence gathering. They can validate or refute sales vision. Finally customers can be a great source of competitor information if they are asked the right way.

At some point, you will want to transition over to a third party for competitive intelligence gathering for two reasons. First, your own people are biased. They are much more likely to point to the competition as the source of price pressure rather than point out that your offering is weak or that sales people are creating price sensitivity through their tactics in the field. Second, as my friend Matt Kelly at Strategy Software puts it: "You can find out virtually anything you want to know about the competition, but gathering the information yourself can border on the unethical and illegal. This is especially the case when it comes to questions about price."[20]

---

[20] Strategy Software specializes in systems for acquiring and utilizing competitive information. www.strategysoftware.com

Value Monetization

Monetizing value is the final element in conceptualizing value delivered. It involves understanding your customer's business well enough to have a hypothesis for how your services deliver benefits to your customer's organization, and how those benefits translate into lower costs or higher revenues and margins.

This is often the part of value based pricing where managers get their undies in a bunch. "We can't do value based pricing because we can't understand value with sufficient accuracy." Let me clear this up. Value based pricing is not about accuracy. As we said earlier, it is about information, approach and rules for success. Put three value pricers in a room working on the same problem and you will get different answers. That said, directionally they will formulate similar conclusions.

In most cases it is not that you know exactly how much your services are worth to the customer. Rather you have gone through the necessary work to make a reasonable estimate of the impact, and can see which elements of your services mix pack the biggest punch. It means that you can have an in depth conversation with your customer about the financial impact of your services on their business, and generally have them agree with you.

Value monetization is vital for pricing with behemoth accounts. In the following example, reduced internal support is a key element of your value proposition, representing over half of your services value to the client.

Value Monetization

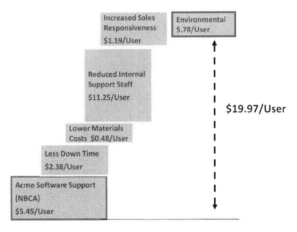

Sure your customer can move to another service supplier, but if they do their costs go up by $11.25 per user per month. For a customer with thousands of users, this cost in total could approach a half million per year.

Truth is your customer may not even see this value in your offering. As we pointed out earlier, value pricing assumes real value and acknowledged value are malleable. It is your responsibility to discover the value and communicate that value to your customer in a meaningful way. Part of the way you communicate that value is capture a price premium for this value delivered. In this case, the company added prices for these technical services to the customer's invoices and then noted that they were granted as part of the current contract.

Design the Offering and Price

Once you have some clarity around value, the next step is offering design. Pricing and offering design go together like Captain Kirk and Mr. Spock. To illustrate the importance of offering design in pricing, let's talk about pricing strategy and defense of the golden goose - maintenance.

The primary risk of maintenance is the size of the pile. Services put together in a pile lose their differentiation, making value difficult to justify. And a large golden pile of undifferentiated services makes an attractive target for corporate budget cutters or competitors.

Let's say that pressure on maintenance is building. You already have a dedicated sales effort, with good tools and training, where people are paid to maintain prices. But it is just not working. Conversion rates are slipping. In fact the president of the firm is getting calls from some of your top customers complaining of your strong-arm tactics.

An offering design approach to solving the problem would begin with segmentation. In most cases pressure begins with a well defined segment of customers with a particular problem that manifests in maintenance price pressure. What kinds of customers are being the most vocal? Who is threatening to leave? Who has left? Since the value of maintenance is largely an extension of product value, it makes sense to look at the product. Has something changed with these customers that has reduced the value of the product to them? For example if your software helps firms optimize capacity utilization and the slow economy has created excess capacity, maintenance pressure is not surprising. Has a new product competitor entered to target these firms? Are firms in financial trouble, looking to control costs? Has a third party service provider, comprised of ex employees, burst onto the scene?

If you have identified a group of price sensitive customers and the reason for their price sensitivity, then you move to offering design. Let's say it is a product problem and there are no plans to fix it. In other words, service department, you are on your own. The goal you would like to achieve is continued margin performance even if the revenues are lower. So you would look closely at this segment and how your services create value for the customer. What services within the pile have the highest value? Which have the highest cost to us? You are looking to remove services from the pile (for this segment only) that have low value to the customer but have high cost to you. These are services your customer must trade off to get a lower price, and because the services have low value to them, they are likely to do so.

At this point a little financial modeling probably makes sense. Are you better off with the customer at the lower price or without the customer? What are the broader customer base implications? Can you build effective fences to make this option available to the target companies and not others?

Then if you choose to pursue it, this tradeoff becomes a new price option for customers. This is not a one customer solution. Rather for customers of this type, who meet these criteria in a defined situation, a price policy is set. Sales is trained for the encounter. In sum, you have retooled your service offering for a well defined segment of customers and protected your margins in the process. This is a value based approach to offering design.

Offering design delivers on the promises made by the value propositions. It provides target customers with choices that permit the firm to maintain customer satisfaction while earning a healthy profit. Offering design answers questions like these

- Should you have a single service level agreement or five SLAs?
- Should you have one rate card or two?
- What services should be bundled together, and which should be unbundled?
- What services must be traded off if customers want price concessions?
- What is pricing's role in meeting our segment marketing and financial objectives?

Each of these questions reflects a component of offering design best addressed when your services mix mirrors your conceptualization of value, and how that value varies by segment.

When you think about value, it is important to think broadly of value delivered. Consider these 5 categories of value. Looking at value this way may reveal some advantages you have over the competition that you may not have considered.

1. Service Value – This is the functional value of your service in performing the work. If it is PS in implementation, it is being successful at that. If it is technical support, it is solving the customer's problem.
2. Process Value – This is the value representing ease of doing business. Let's say I have copy machines installed from two manufacturers. When the copier from manufacturer A starts having problems, a secretary has to call the company for service. When the copier from manufacturer B starts having problems, a service call is automatically generated electronically.

No human intervention is involved. This is process value. So even if the service value is the same, i.e. both machines are repaired equally quickly and at the same price, this process value of less effort and speedier ordering has value.

3. <u>Relationship Value</u> – This is the value that two companies create through working together. The Intel Inside sticker on my laptop confers relationship value to the manufacturer's laptop.

4. <u>Social Value</u> – This value has become more important over the last decade as investors have pressured companies to consider the broader societal impacts of their business. In the chemical industry, for example, some companies have a green reputation. Others might be characterized as decidedly brown.

5. <u>Brand Value</u> – Companies invest a lot into their brand. This degree of affinity for the brand also has value.

OFFERING CONFIGURATION

OK. I threw in the golden goose maintenance example above to get your attention. Now I am going to add a little sauce to make it even more tasty. If you subscribe to the notion that value added services are the future of tech, then this chapter is for you. I will give you a process that describes how to design value added services. So drop and give me 20, and when you are awake keep reading.

Services offering configuration begins with segmentation. Even if you deliver exactly the same product to segment after segment, how that product is used by customers in each segment will be different. So service offering configuration begins with understanding what services are needed by each segment and why. This understanding creates natural breaks around which a services mix can be built. In the value monetization example above, the value of internal support staff suggests a natural break. Some customers get that benefit and pay for it. Others don't and don't.

An important cut in offering configuration is degree of difference in service needs across segments. To the degree value delivered is similar across all segments, the services mix needed will be common across all segments. This becomes your core offering. In a PS environment, this is your minimal implementation package. With service agreements, this is your minimum service agreement package.

To the degree service needs are different across segments, service options are needed. This is not the precious metals approach of bronze, silver, gold, platinum, which suggests there is a linear progression of service needs across segments. Nothing could be further from the truth. There is nothing linear about the needs of different segments. Each segment has different needs, so service packages are tailored to them. If similar services happen to be sought by different segments, so be it, but that's not where you start.

For example, you may have a group of customers who is determined to be self sufficient in their use of your products. As a result, your service package for them works to make them best at self sufficiency. Note, they don't want a low level of service. Instead they want to be excellent at self sufficiency. You deliver the highest value and potentially the highest margin by helping them be self sufficient.

Alternatively you may have another customer group who doesn't want to think about how your products work, they simply want to maximize throughput and minimize downtime. This is managed services. It is not that customers want a high level of service, rather they want a solution that delivers targeted KPI performance. Value and margins are potentially highest if you deliver what they want.

Consider the implications of each of these cases for cost management. In each case we have decoupled price from cost, and attached price to the customer's objectives. In the first case, if we can automate the delivery of services to support self reliance, we can drive costs down and expand margins while the customer is happy to pay. In the second case, managed services, if we can keep the KPI high we can lower our costs of delivery as much as we want. Customer is happy and our margins grow.

The following graphic illustrates a generic offering design and price menu for technology services.

Offering Design & Price Menu

	Targeted VAS Bundle1	Targeted VAS Bundle 2	Targeted VAS Bundle 3	Ala Carte	AC Prices
	Role based learning paths	Release Readiness Reports	Remote Monitoring	Remote Monitoring	$12,000
	Online training	Developer Support	24 x 7 support	Developer Support	$12,000
	24 hour response	4 hour response	Success Resource	24/7 Support	$15,000
	Onboarding Consulting	Assigned Resource		Success Resource	?20,000
				Online Training	$5,000
Price	$25,000	$45,000	$65,000		

Core Offering (ES Bundle)				CO Price
Online Case Submission	3 day response	Customer Community	Training (4 basic courses)	12% of SW Price

Base Offering				BO Price
FAQ	N/A	N/A	N/A	0

Copyright 2013, Timothy Matanovich

In my view, the offering and price menu needs to have four distinct parts.

1. Core Offering – This is the set of services that you strongly recommend for all customers. This is a one price fits all model, though the price level may vary based on scale of implementation.

2. Base Offering – Some customers may just be knuckleheads and insist on buying your product without support. Your base offering is the set of services that you insist on no matter what the customer says.

3. Target VAS Bundle Offerings – These are bundled service packages targeted to segments of customers with common sets of needs. These are value added services. The price of the VAS bundles is typically less than the price of the services included if purchased ala carte.

4. Ala Carte Offerings – Some customers may have unique needs or simply are stubborn blocks (my dad's favorite description of me) and want to buy offerings ala carte. Priced individually, these prices are typically highest and should encourage customers to buy bundles.

In a world governed by consumption economics, where users choose services as their capabilities grow, it may be appropriate to add a second level of segmentation based on the customer's value chain. For example, your utilization monitoring suggests an accounting team may be ready for advanced functionality. This is an incremental package of services that can be presented to targeted customers to determine if they want to make it available.

An important characteristic of technology services pricing is the mechanics of service pricing must play well with the mechanics of product pricing. From the customer's perspective it is all of a piece. Pricing of that offering therefore should be internally consistent and easy to understand. That is not to say that service prices should be set as a percent of product price. With essential services, the practice may make sense. Maintenance is a perfect example. But products commoditize faster than services, service economics may be fundamentally different than product economics and service value gets lost when bundled. In these cases prices should be detached and the menu should reflect this detachment.

Now you have an offering design and price menu that will be intelligible to both managmeent and sales people alike. This menu permits sales people to have conversations with customers about options available and to negotiate tradeoffs without caving on price. Customers can purchase high value or no value as they choose. Designed well, you make money no matter what your customer chooses.

This is essential to negotiation strategy. When customers demand a price concession, how do you respond? If your offering is rigid, you have no choice but to lower price. You are in a stronger negotiating position if you have a flexible offering so that service elements can be removed from the mix. This was the maintenance defense described earlier. If a customer wants a lower price, fine, they get fewer services. The goal is that revenues may go up or down, but margin remains intact.

Consider offering configuration as the balancing of several factors in order to create a win-win negotiation with your customers.

- Services valued similarly across all segments define your essential service offering. These are the services you recommend, perhaps insist, all customers buy.
- Services valued differently across segments create natural breaks for offering design. For example, these become the differentiators that

justify price differences across SLA packages. These define your value added services.

- Services with high differential value position you most powerfully with the customer. These should represent the core of your value proposition, e.g. the two or three elements of your service mix that really make a difference to customers in the target segment. These services are the heart of your value added services.

- Services with high costs should form the basis for your value tradeoffs. If customers push you for lower prices, fine. Don't let them push down your margins. High value, high cost services are particularly useful in negotiations because they force the customer to feel the pain of the lower price.[21]

- Finally, there may be other considerations. For tech firms employing a product provider strategy in a rapidly growing market, 90% of the firm's attention is on the product, and rightly so. Service configuration may be limited to essential services.

In sum, offering configuration is not linear, not precious metals and not rigid. It is about packaging your services to exactly meet the needs of target customer segments, thereby creating the highest value for them and the highest overall margin for your company. It is about decoupling value to the customer and cost to serve. It is about building in flexibility so that sales can ask for value concessions in exchange for price concessions.

---

[21] Note this remains win-win negotiation. If we have done our homework, the customer is better off paying a higher price and worse off with a lower price. We want them to feel the pain of their shortsighted decision.

SERVICES PRICING STRATEGIES

Price drives behavior among customers, competitors and our sales organization. It is one of the three legs of marketing strategy. It is arguably the single most powerful communication we have with our customers. It is the nuclear warhead of the marketing arsenal. It is the single most powerful driver of profitability. Any questions? As a result, make no mistake, pricing is at the heart of business strategy.

In the next chapter of this book we will dive deeply into services pricing strategy. My objective here is to focus on the three fundamental pricing strategies.

Reflect back on the customer segmentation. There we identified groups of customers that varied along the following dimensions.

1. High Volume Producers
2. Solution Providers
3. Economic Impact of Downtime
4. Internal Technical Support Capabilities

To illustrate, let's extend the example given above about a customer segment who is a self reliant solution provider. You have configured a services bundle for them because your pricing consultant told you to. So what is your strategy? This customer group is not very large, but they are potentially very profitable.

The only way they can maintain their self reliance is by using your company as a single supplier, just like Southwest Airlines maintains its cost advantage by exclusively using Boeing 737s. They want top notch training for their people, tailored to their unique needs. They not only need formal classroom training,

114

but they need access to just-in-time online training that meets the ongoing needs of their people as they develop and grow. Your services have become part of their culture. Switching costs are high because productivity could be lost for a year or more by changing suppliers. When they call us, they need our Level 3 support which is our highest margin service. Because it is level 3 support, they get outstanding service.

The pricing strategy for this segment might be charging a price premium to maximize profitability. Actually a price premium is a bargain for these customers because they handle most of the services themselves. So we make very high margins on the few services they use. Because they are intensely trained and accustomed to level 3 support, they become excellent references. In addition, we can see a movement to the cloud in our future. These self reliant customers are lead users who can show us how to develop services for other self reliant cloud customers.

Customers that experience little immediate financial impact from downtime would look at the world differently. They might have their needs met by Level 1 or Level 2 support. This might be 25% of the customer base. For these customers, a third party might even provide adequate levels of support. Switching costs are lower. As a result, a lower, more competitive price might be in order. Given the size of the segment, these customers permit you to achieve services economies of scale. These economies make your service operations efficient overall and permit you to earn a profit even at a lower price.

Business strategy may also have implications broader than the service organization. We talked about substitution and complementary service effects earlier. Prices for consultants in residency for a year are typically 10% lower than prices for consultants more broadly. This preferred pricing may make sense for two reasons.

1. Costs drop rapidly with higher utilization, making it possible to earn a higher profit with a lower price.
2. Resident consultants are better situated to identify new product and service opportunities, so a tradeoff in price is more than offset by a rise in complimentary product and service sales.

In each of these cases, pricing strategy leads business strategy. In general ask yourself whether a premium, neutral or penetration strategy makes sense. Ask how this pricing strategy supports your broader business strategy. Finally ask how this pricing strategy supports the underlying economics of the business.

Three Basic Pricing Strategies

Skim pricing involves capturing high margins at the expense of sales volume. Skim makes sense when your people have highly specialized skills or your service organization has unique capabilities that are not easily duplicated, and this specialization and uniqueness are highly valued by a segment of customers. Skim pricing may involve some risk because customers may react negatively if they perceive the high prices as unfair.

Penetration pricing involves keeping price low in order to attract and hold a large base of customers. Penetration pricing works well where variable costs are low and where the incremental cost of attracting and holding those customers is small relative to the price. Each incremental sale, then, adds a substantial contribution to profit. Penetration pricing in services may make sense when services are highly automated and self directed, i.e. where the majority of underlying costs are fixed and incremental costs per customer are low. Penetration pricing can involve substantial financial risk when the underlying costs are higher than anticipated. Penetration pricing can also lead to a price war when it is interpreted by competitors as price aggression.

Neutral pricing is the decision not to use price to either grow margin or grow share. Neutral pricing may make sense when the downsides of using skim or penetration pricing is greater than the potential upsides.

DECIDE PRICE LEVELS

With the menu structured, the remaining decision is how much to charge. Deciding the price level for technology services involves four steps: deciding the price range, evaluating price sensitivity, deciding the strategic price level and deciding on a price metric.

PRICE RANGE

Too often managers paint themselves into a corner on price by going directly to a target price without considering how much flexibility they actually have. The price range is simply a range of possible prices the firm could reasonably charge for a service given an estimate of value created and competitive alternatives. The high end of the price range is typically the

> *Too often managers paint themselves into a corner on price by going directly to target price without considering how much flexibility they actually have.*

value delivered. Customers won't pay more than value delivered unless they have a gun to their head or are deceived. On the low end, the range is defined by the price of a competitive alternative. If your primary professional services competitor is the client's internal staff, then that is the low end of the range. For example, a service package might have a potential price range of $200,000 to $400,000. Using this price range as a starting point opens the pricing conversation up to possibilities.

PRICE SENSITIVITY

The next step is to consider price sensitivity. For example, in many cases customer price sensitivity for professional services is high at the time of software purchase and much lower at the time of service only upgrades. This is particularly true in cases where the size of the PS budget is large relative to the software price. In other cases I have seen the exact opposite. When PS budget is modest compared to the product price, there is little price sensitivity to the PS price. I don't know what your situation is, but as you consider the price range, ask yourself: What should our prices be in these different buying situations? How can our menu be structured to reflect these differences?

Typically price sensitivity rises in situations where alternatives are known and easy to compare, where the price represents a sizable expenditure by the customer, when the brand is weak or where switching costs are low. By contrast, price sensitivity drops when alternatives are not well understood and are difficult to compare, where the expenditure is not sizable, when the brand is strong and where switching costs are high.

An in depth discussion of price sensitivity permits managers to identify situations when it might be possible to capture a higher price, and situations where being more competitive with price is called for. The discussion should also reveal actions the firm can take to reduce sensitivity. For example, presenting a T&M budget to customers always makes them more price sensitive than when they are presented with a fixed fee budget. How can you manage the inherent risk of a PS engagement while simultaneously reaping the upside potential fixed fee presents?

Consider a prospect you are working with right now. What can you do to make your offering more difficult to compare to the competition? What can you do to manage the switching costs in your favor? What can you do to invest in the strength of your brand – <u>specifically related to services</u>? This is where packaged IP can dramatically improve margin performance.

High price sensitivity suggests your offering price should be at the lower end of the band. Low price sensitivity suggests your price should be higher. The discussion of price sensitivity narrows the range of acceptable prices within the price band.

PRICE LEVEL DECISIONS

Your basic pricing strategy – skim, penetrate or neutral – combined with your assessment of sensitivity permit you to decide on an appropriate price level. In actuality, this can be a tough decision. Product managers, sales, pricing, executives often come to the table with different agendas. As mentioned above, there is no right answer. If you have been diligent through the process, however, your ultimate price decision will be good enough.

PRICE METRIC

A price metric is a measurable operating characteristic of a customer that ties your price to the value delivered, permitting easy scaling. In technology services, for example, companies vary price based on number of seats, number of members, percent of product or license price, number of inquiries and number of boxes. In gain share arrangements, the service provider and customer decide on KPIs that determine how the value of the services is shared between them.

To be most useful, price metrics should be easy to measure, straightforward to interpret and difficult to manipulate.

APPENDIX: MARKET BASED PRICING

Many firms practice market based pricing. Though it is not part of PTSP, it is better than cost based pricing. In some cases, market based pricing makes perfect sense to pursue. The following section is intended for market based pricers who want to up their game.

As described earlier in the chapter on Pricing Belief Systems, a market based pricing approach assumes there is a market price for a service offering and the goal of pricing is to match the market. We also pointed out that a common tool used in setting market based pricing is a market map. Let's use a software implementation case study to demonstrate market mapping and market based pricing.

MARKET MAPPING - ACME PHARMACEUTICALS

The software license purchase has been completed, and our client is a U.S. drug manufacturer, making the decision about how best to implement. Essentially she has 4 options.

1. Build it themselves using their in-house staff
2. Hire a local PS firm to install the software
3. Hire a national/international PS firm that is an expert in their industry (pharmaceuticals)
4. Hire the PS staff from the software company

The choice is not easy. Each of the alternatives brings different strengths to the table. If she builds it herself, she will likely have the lowest out-of-pocket expenses, but with competing priorities, implementation time could take years. She has used a local consulting firm in the past for a variety of engagements, but this would be the biggest project they have ever been asked to tackle. The industry experts would likely bring state of the art processes with them, but they are expensive and their processes may not conform to the software without added customization. Finally, the software firm's consultants are the most expensive, but they would be able to get her project up and running in the shortest time.

So how does she make the choice? Even if we had perfect knowledge of competitors' prices in this case, we would still be at a loss to predict her behavior. Obviously we need to understand the relative value side of the equation as well. If we understand the relative value of the alternatives and their relative prices, we could understand her choice.

Exhibit 6 is a Market Map of her options. Market maps are powerful tools for understanding price and value positions of competitors and for establishing and refining pricing and competitive strategy. On the vertical axis is perceived price. On the horizontal axis is perceived value. Over time competitive factors in the market and customer preferences force competitors to line up along the diagonal in a discontinuous fashion. Price points usually reflect clusters of competitors who have a specific value profile. This array of the competitors is intuitively obvious. In short: you get what you pay for.

Professional Services
Market Map Example

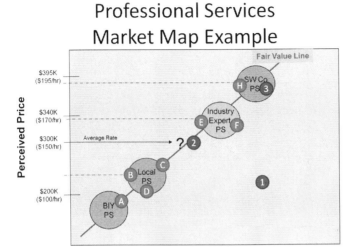

If the market is at equilibrium, then all competitors line up along the "Fair Value Line". In this case, the software company PS has improved its value position without changing its price, and is located to the right of the line, disrupting the equilibrium. Other players in the market will ultimately react to the software company, in an attempt to restore equilibrium. Value and price positions are in constant motion, as competitors vie for clients.

In reality, we would expect to see a PS team comprised of a variety of job titles at different numbers of hours. For simplicity sake here, let's say the team is 5 people, priced at the specified blended rate. Software company consultants are priced the highest, near $200 per hour and local consultants are lowest at $100. Industry Experts are priced at roughly $170 per hour.

Returning to our pharma industry buyer, she is largely indifferent to the competitors on the line. If she paid $340K for industry experts, she would get good value for the price. If she paid $240K for local consultants, she would get good value at that price. If we make the assumption that she is a value buyer, willing to pay more for value received, and that she does not have constraints on her budget, then the software company team offers the best return on her investment, though she will pay them the highest price, roughly $395K. In this case the software company wins the business.

Notice that the average price is $200. Looking at the Market map, there are no competitors at that price. That may suggest that there are no customers willing to buy services from a PS company that is not quite an industry expert and too expensive to be a local provider. Alternatively it may suggest that there is a pool of customers that would be willing to pay that price but are currently underserved by existing suppliers. Again we need information about value preferences of buyers to determine whether a $200 price is a good idea or a disaster waiting to happen.

Throughout the market mapping discussion, I referred repeatedly to perceived value and perceived price. These are important concepts, instrumental to creating and applying this powerful tool.

Perceived value is easiest to understand. When our Pharma buyer researched the PS alternatives available she was likely bombarded with marketing and sales materials from the various companies, not to mention industry research studies and conversations with her peers and colleagues. In total, this is probably hundreds (if not thousands) of pages of material. Naturally, unless she is like my photographic memory friend George, she won't be able to remember it all. More than likely during the learning process she will begin creating a list of key offering benefits and attributes that form the basis of her choice. In many cases, these result in the requirements document.

For most of us, the list we can keep track of is pretty short – 3-7 factors. We simply can't remember more. These are the value factors that determine how she rank orders and chooses among the competitors. Essentially she has built herself a mental map of the competitive market. And when it comes to choosing a PS supplier, she wants answers to three basic questions

1. How well will this work when implementation is completed?
2. How easy are they to do business with?
3. Is this a company I can count on into the future?

On the other side of the equation is perceived price, a more difficult concept. As much as your sales people might argue to the contrary, the buyer is likely to be just as confused about competitor pricing as you are. In this case, she will get three different proposals, each for different work with different price levels and structures. Plus she has her own build-it-yourself budget. She probably has experience working in the past with a number of suppliers, and so has some expectations of what can be had for what money. Finally, she has probably received some input from finance on what monies are available and their sources.

Again, with all the input she has received, she can't keep track of it all. The perceived price is the expectation she has for price level and structure from a given type of competitor. If a proposal comes in and is out of whack with her expectations, high or low, that competitor may very well face early elimination.

Putting value and price together, the market map is a mental map of customers in the market place. Perceived value is the expected set of benefits from different suppliers. Perceived price is the expected prices she expects to pay to those suppliers. To be a player with a chance at winning, a PS supplier must meet the value and price expectations of the client. As one of the competitors, what you really want to know is what's on her list and how you stack up relative to the competition on both value and price.

On the pricing axis, price may be a combination of factors working together. The set of factors you include in the analysis will depend on how your customer looks at the lifetime costs of using your services.

- Initial Price – This is the initial out of pocket price for the service.
- Operating Cost – This is the month to month cost of availing oneself of the service.
- Switching Costs – This is the one-time cost to the company of moving from use of one offering to the next.

MARKET MAPPING ADVANTAGES & SHORTCOMINGS

The great advantage of market mapping is ease of use. If you are in a market with a number of competitors and established offerings, you have the raw material to create a map. In fairly short order a management team can think through advantages and disadvantages relative to competitors and build a map. Research or data mining can be used to backfill and validate. The map makes price-value segments obvious. If you are a cost based pricer, market based pricing is directionally correct. Market mapping reveals price segments and positioning. The factors that underly the map, and the weighting scheme used, provide insights for service investment, value propositions and sales effort. Finally, market maps are great communication tools. They are easy to understand and interpret, are useful for exploring strategic alternatives and plotting competitive strategies.

RED OCEAN THINKING – A MARKET BASED PRICING SHORTCOMING

One of the best strategy books of the last decade is Blue Ocean Strategy. In the book the authors describe red oceans where competitive rules are well defined and competitors engage in a bloody battle for share. As an alternative, they suggest businesses create blue oceans by looking at markets in unique ways and where you define the rules of competition and thus limit the competitive forces you face. market based pricing is useful for pricing in red oceans, but is largely useless for pricing when you are looking to create blue oceans.[22]

Market based pricing looks primarily toward the competition to determine what value is and can be. Revisiting the Surfboard, as a result of this competitor orientation Acknowledged Value is perceived to be largely fixed, i.e. the market has already decided what value can be delivered and what price it is willing to pay. The factors governing competition are well defined and the relationships are linear. So as a method for pricing existing services, particularly essential services, market based pricing is useful.

On the other hand, as a method for pricing new services, value added services or for considering game changing services, market based pricing falls short. Service value may be thought of in three categories.

1. Required - Customers will not buy from any competitor unless these services are included.
2. Nice to have - Customers might pay us a little more for these services

---

[22] W. Chan Kim and Renee Maurborgne, Blue Ocean Strategy: How to create uncontested market space and make the competition irrelevant

3. Meaningfully Differentiated - Customers will choose us over the competition because our services are unique and directly impact the customer's business model.

The real kicker is number 3. If you are looking to create competitive advantage with customers through meaningfully differentiated services, and you want to capture a fair share of the value you create, market based pricing is of limited use.

BEHEMOTH ACCOUNTS – AN MARKET BASED PRICING SHORTCOMING

If you are pricing into a market with many customers, then market based pricing may work. It gets you into the ballpark and gives you a shot at winning. But what about that big account that represents half of your revenues. The one that loves everything that you provide and then sics their Klingon procurement staff on you to cut the lowest price. How do you defend prices or ideally capture value at those accounts?

To succeed at pricing with behemoth accounts, you need to understand why they need you and how much you are worth to them. What is it that you deliver that your competitors don't? Why is it they consistently choose you? What is the business impact that your services have

> *To succeed at pricing with behemoth accounts, you need to understand why they need you and how much you are worth to them. Market based pricing underestimates the value of differentiation. It will not tell you that a 2% change in benefits results in a 100X reduction in operating costs.*

that your competitors' don't? None of those questions is clearly answered through market based pricing.

Market based pricing underestimates the value of differentiation. For example, a market map may tell you that your service offers twice the benefits of your competitor. It will not tell you that a 2X change in benefits results in a 100X reduction in your customer's operating costs.

MEASURING PRICE ELASTICITY – A MARKET BASED PRICING SHORTCOMING

Market based pricing is notoriously inadequate as a model for measuring price elasticity. As noted, market based pricing is good to get you in the right ballpark, but it provides no insight into whether a price increase will be accepted without adverse reaction. More, if an adverse reaction is to be expected, market based pricing can't help you judge how much it will be.

Alternatively, value based pricing (value based pricing) approach helps you answer the question in two ways. First, since elasticity is primarily determined by the relationship between price and value, it provides a ready scale for evaluating the elasticity question. The closer the price asked is to value delivered, the less incentive there is for customers to buy and therefore higher elasticity. On the other hand, the greater the gap between price and value delivered, i.e. high incentive to buy, the lower the elasticity.

Second, a value based pricing approach recognizes that buyers with different needs value the same offering differently. So raising your prices may have no impact with one set of customers, but may prompt you to lose business with a second set of customers. Value based pricing permits you to visualize how a price change might shift demand between segments and thereby estimate the impact of a price change.

EXECUTIONAL WEAKNESS – A MARKET BASED PRICING SHORTCOMING

So you have mapped a new service offering relative to the competition and have decided on a market based pricing by triangulating between competitors. How do you configure the offering and pricing menu? Consider these questions.

1. What services should be included in the core service bundle for all customers?

2. What services meaningfully differentiate your offering to different segments?

3. How should prices be set for these services?

4. What services should you pull out of a bundle as a value tradeoff if the customer demands a lower price?

5. How should you structure your service mix so that customers don't migrate to the low priced option?

6. What services should you be willing to trade off easily during negotiations?

7. How do you answer all these questions in a way that justifies pricing to sales, and helps them better communicate and negotiate with customers?

Because market based pricing is competitor oriented and uses tools like market maps as proxies for value, the results tend to be output that is pretty good, i.e. directionally correct, but lacking the details necessary to set the stage for effective price execution by the sales organization. Is it useful for sales? Yes. Does it provide sales with tools and processes for capturing price? Largely no.

In sum, market based pricing is a step in the right direction if you start by abandoning the idea that there is a "market price" out there that provides a common reference for all competitors. It is strategic, relatively easy to use, is easy to communicate and is directionally correct in setting price. At its best it tries to emulate value based pricing. As for shortcomings, market based pricing is limited in its ability to set price for new to the world services or value added services. It is largely useless for pricing to behemoth accounts and for evaluating price elasticity. Finally, market based pricing is weak in setting the stage for sales and pricing executional success.

"Gentlemen, let's broaden our minds."
-   Joker

CHAPTER 6 - SERVICES PRICING STRATEGY

If you have made it this far, I am truly impressed. The last two chapters might have been alternatively titled: Eat Your Spinach and Eat Your Brussels Sprouts. They were really good for you, but probably not your favorites. Well, that is going to change here. This is a nice rib-eye, grilled just perfect. Tastes great and you will get your day's protein.

The entire premise for this book is that technology services pricing requires unique treatment. As described in the chapter on objectives, this uniqueness derives from the dynamism of the environment, services intangibility, the array of services, regulatory requirements and the variety of pricing methods. In sum: complexity. To effectively manage price in this environment, therefore, requires a framework that creates simplicity from the chaos. A useful framework will reflect the market reality and customer behaviors we observe, encompass the full range of technology services and provide guidance for decision making.

From the company's internal perspective, services fall into two broad categories: structured and unstructured. This is the way firms tend to organize themselves. Structured services are packaged for consumption. Examples include maintenance, warranty, SLAs, training and even predefined implementation services. These services have a fixed price that is defined in advance of the sale. Unstructured services are represented by professional services such as implementation, integration, field services, often priced by the hour, process reengineering or business consulting. Unstructured services are customized to the needs of an individual customer and the price is determined during the sales process.

From the customer's perspective, the view is a bit different. Services are viewed through the lens of what is important to them. Some services are part of their cost stream. These are costs they must incur though there is no clear benefit to the service. Other services are part of their value stream where there is a clear connection between the services delivered and their business success. In TS terminology these are called essential services and value added services.

Essential services are necessary for the successful utilization of technology. For example, implementation services are necessary to install software onto a customer's systems. Software that is not implemented is "shelfware" and produces zero benefits for the customer's organization. Likewise maintenance is necessary to sustain the software's value over its useful life.

Value added services, on the other hand, are viewed as discretionary purchases by customers. Value added services don't simply enable utilization, they permit a customer to optimize it. Second or third tier SLAs are good examples. Customers pay a price premium for selected service bundles. Business process reengineering is another example that focuses on optimizing business processes around a system.

So how do you determine which is which – ES vs. VAS? The following exhibit provides the answer.

What are Value Added Services?

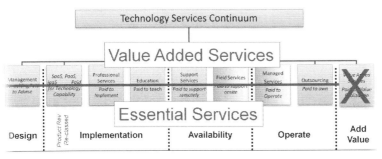

Adapted from : TSIA

Any service from management consulting through outsourcing can be either an essential service or a value added service. Which it is depends on decisions you make about the product-service relationship and the customers you target. This is a key idea, so I am going to say it one more time. The only difference between an essential service and a value added service is the decisions you make about the product-service relationship and the customers you target.[23]

For those of you who think in color, in your management decisions you need to draw a big fat red line between essential and value added services because how you market and price these two services will be radically different.

---

[23] If you didn't pay attention the first two times, here it is again. Any service can be either essential or value add. If you want to get paid for value added services you need to make different decisions about the product-service relationship and the customers you target.

THE TS PRICING STRATEGY MATRIX

The TS Pricing Strategy Matrix uses the internal and external perspective of services to create a framework to guide pricing strategy decisions. This framework can be used to both explain pricing behaviors that we observe as well as suggest paths for improving price performance. The names in each cell characterize the appropriate pricing strategy for that cell.

Profitable Technology Services Pricing™

3. Services Pricing Strategy

How do we integrate service pricing and product pricing?

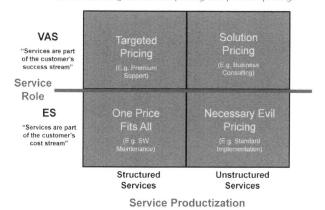

NECESSARY EVIL PRICING

Let's start with basic implementation as an example of an unstructured, necessary service. Consider a typical implementation of a software or hardware product. What value does the implementation itself add above and beyond the product being installed? The answer is zero. Implementation adds no value, it simply permits the product value to be realized. What the customer wants is the functionality of the product. If they could get that

138

functionality without the implementation, they would happily do it. Unfortunately for customers, they have to go through the pain of implementation to avail themselves of the product benefits. So in this quadrant, professional services pricing is simply a necessary evil.

Thinking about unstructured, essential services pricing as a necessary evil explains much of the behavior we observe inside tech companies. Sales is focused on the product because the product holds all the value. That's what the customer wants to buy. There is high pressure from sales to lower the price of these services because they add no value of themselves and are impossible to justify. Customers also keep a close eye on these budgets.

The problem from the company's standpoint is that these services are expensive and must be paid for. The product must be custom fit into the buyer's organization. Since there is no value to the services, value is not negotiated. Instead scope and price are negotiated. Sometimes companies give away these services, but the costs usually make this prohibitive over the long run.

Fortunately, the supplier has the customer over a barrel. If they want the benefits of the product they must pay for the implementation. So the goal is to price implementation services to be "acceptable" to the customer. Cost based pricing works. It is straightforward and can be justified. Market based pricing is better because it is similarly straightforward and easily justified, with the added benefit that market prices for these services are routinely higher than cost based prices.

Necessary evil pricing also explains the risk to PS organizations from the entry of Products as a Service into their market space. Customers get the benefits of the product without having to pay for the pain of implementation. Given the high cost of implementation and the lack of value contribution, customers have a great incentive to switch to XaaS when they are shopping for new systems.

ONE SIZE FITS ALL PRICING

Shifting left in our matrix, we come to the next essential service category: structured, essential services. Examples include maintenance, warranty and basic training services. These are the service levels that suppliers argue are necessary for all customers to utilize. This is a key concept, so before you read further, splash cold water on your face, take a shot of 5 Hour Energy, do 22 jumping jacks, do whatever you need to do to pay attention.

Maintenance is the insurance plan that every customer must have to assure that the software continues to deliver benefits and value over time. Price may be scaled for size of customer, but the price is essentially the same for all customers. With minor variations, for example, every license software customer pays 20% of the license price for maintenance – one size fits all pricing.

Now here is a key concept: Structured essential services are defined by the customer with the lowest level of needs. By definition these services are essential so everybody, including your lowliest customer, should have them. If you have ten customers and you rank ordered them by service needs, essential services would be defined by number 10.

This doesn't mean few services in an absolute sense. Perhaps you are Cray, providing very high end systems with very stringent support requirements. Then essential services are still defined by your lowest need customers. It's just that low in this case is not very low. In the earlier section on developing a price menu, these are your "Core Services".

Core services are not the same as commodity services. Rather it is a management decision. Based on your customers and how you want to position your offering versus competitors, you decide on the set of services that you recommend all customers have? This may be different than your competitors and so is not a commodity.

Why is this concept of setting your base services for your lowliest customers so important? It is vitally important for pricing because there is a lot more money to be made from the added value needed by the other 9 customers. If you bundle these higher value services together with essential services, their value gets lost in the pile.

Experience across many industries has shown that services easily lose their differentiated value when bundled. It has to do with the intangibility of services. Products retain their individuality in bundles, e.g. it is easy to differentiate between fries and a burger even when served as a Happy Meal. In contrast, tell me what are the individual services in your auto insurance policy? Beyond one or two services most of us couldn't list them; that despite the fact that they are the most

> *If you bundle higher value services together with essential services, their value gets lost in the pile.*

important components of the policies and we pay hundreds of times more for auto insurance than we do for a Happy Meal. Then in times of natural disaster it is no surprise that so many people discover that their insurance didn't cover the flood or hail or wind or other damage. Services lose differentiation in bundles.

So in order to capture maximum value in services, unbundling has proven an effective pricing tactic. Itemizing services more clearly communicates value. Providing customers with more options generally increases customer spend. Unbundling is especially important for new value added services. The last thing you want to do is develop something truly valuable for your customers and then bury it in a pile of other services under the label "maintenance".

Another trap of indiscriminant bundling is competitive vulnerability. A favorite competitive strategy since the time of Sun Tzu has been to narrowly define the field of battle in order to gain relative competitive strength. Working across a variety of industries, time and again niche competitors attack the highest margin elements of an incumbent's undifferentiated offering. Continuing the insurance industry example, there has been a flurry of activity in the auto insurance industry recently led by Progressive and Geico. "Name your own price", "choose the policy that is right for you", and "do it for less money". It is a powerful combination. Note recently that industry powerhouses like Allstate and State Farm have been forced to follow suit. In software, SaaS is a direct fontal attack on the profit pool known as maintenance.

Now let's move to value. What is the value of maintenance? As with implementation services, the incremental value of maintenance is zero. The value is in the product's functionality and delivered benefits. If customers could buy software that worked well over time, and they had no switching costs, they would drop maintenance like a hot potato. It has no value in its own right. So perhaps the way to think about the maintenance price is that it is a component of the product price. In pricing terminology this would be known as a two-part tariff, e.g. 50% up front and 50% over the next 5 years.

Let's jump to warranty services for a minute to generalize the principle. When a customer purchases a product they expect it to deliver its benefits and do so for a defined lifespan. This may be 15 minutes in the case of a Starbucks paper cup, 25 years for an aircraft engine and something in between for your favorite hardware. A warranty is a structured, essential service with the price of zero. It is essential because customers would not buy the product without it.[24] Is there a price the customer pays for this service? Yes, but it is subsumed in the product price. One price fits all. It is just the one price that fits all happens to be zero.

TARGETED PRICING

What do you do with the services you pulled out of the pile? The answer is make money off them with targeted pricing. Let's return to our 10 customers. Only one of them, suspect number 10, has had his needs fully met. The others remain hungry for more. Aren't you glad now I moved from spinach and Brussels Sprouts to steak?

---

[24] Note that lack of implied warranty is the exception, usually written on a sign in big red letters

Actually, hungry is a good metaphor. If these 9 people were a typical mix and you asked them where they would like to go out for dinner, 4 might say Macaroni Grill, 3 might say the Yard House and the remaining two would split between Ruth Cris and Old Chicago. The point is we all have different tastes. When you move from essential services to value added services (VAS) you are moving from a pool of money customers feel they must spend to a pool of money they choose to spend. You are moving from a set of services that are seen as part of their cost stream to a set of services they see as part of their success stream.

More coffee now. Splash water on your face. Value added services are not simply an extension of essential services. They are a radical departure from essential services. From a sales perspective, services organizations have had it easy. Essential services sell themselves. The customer must pay for them or they don't get the benefits and value of the product. Sure, customers dicker over the price, but they know at the end of the day essential

> *When you move from essential services to value added services you are moving from a pool of money customers feel they must spend to a pool of money they choose to spend.*

services are, well, essential. Value added services must be proactively marketed and sold. Essential services don't need marketing. Value added services not only need marketing, they need a marketing strategy.

Once upon a time I worked with a firm that sold software and services to collection agencies. Since all collectors have essentially the same job, using the same tools with the same performance metrics, the core software product and essential services were the same across all customers. The collection process, however, varied significantly across type of debt, usually based on legal requirements. Credit cards required one process, medical collections another, cars another and home another. In other words, there are target segments of buyers with unique needs. The pricing for the basic software and essential services was one price fits all, but the incremental price for value added services and software were priced based on the value delivered to these individual segments.

How high might these targeted value added services be priced? My perspective is that the sky is the limit. About a third of the country subscribes to DirecTV with subscription prices in the range of $79-129 per month. Then comes along a pay-per-view fight that you can't live without and you pay $59 for at most 2 hours. So you are moving from an hourly rate of 36 cents to an hourly rate of nearly $30. That is 100X higher for the value added services. That's the power of targeted pricing.

Actually DirecTV is an outstanding example of targeted pricing. Think of all the ways DirecTV gives you to spend more money. There are these one-time special events. There are upgraded movie packages. There are pay per view for TV shows and movies, some cheap and some expensive. You can add high speed internet. Don't forget about sports packages. And there are probably more. Targeted pricing to the max.

SOLUTION PRICING

So far we have seen that unstructured, essential services like PS implementation call for Necessary Evil Pricing. Structured essential services, like maintenance, require One Size Fits All Pricing. Structured, value added services, like third tier SLAs require Targeted Pricing. In the final quadrant we ask the question: how should we price unstructured services like consulting when they don't just enable the product value, but when they create unique value of their own? The answer is Solution Pricing.

Why do companies hire consultants for thousands of dollars per day? What is the value add? The answer is to improve business performance and solve problems. And why would they choose unstructured services like professional services? The answer is because the problem they need to solve requires exceptional skills in diagnostics, discovering value, configuring solutions, selling, and driving change.

These consultants may sell products, but they do so in the context of working collaboratively with a client to solve a problem where they are paid not only for the products, but the glue that holds them together, the solution. Like the quadrant immediately below, where consultants provide essential services, the target is the single company you are working with. From there, however, things change dramatically. With implementation, for example, the likely buyer is the CIO. With solutions, the likely buyer is a business buyer. With implementation, scope and price are discovered and negotiated. In solution pricing, value and price are discovered and negotiated. With implementation, sales is focused on selling the product. With solutions, product sales people don't have the necessary skills. PS needs its own highly skilled sales force with the ability to discover and sell the unique value that consultants bring as distinct from product value.

Even more coffee now. Splash water on your face. Down some NoXplode. Do a Tabata workout. I am going to make the same argument I made for Targeted Pricing above. The distinction is that Solution Pricing is that the target market for solutions is a target of one, a single customer. Value added professional services are not simply an extension of essential professional services. They are a radical departure. From the PS organization's perspective they have had it easy. Essential services sell themselves. It may feel like war in the trenches, but what real choice does the customer have? The customer must pay for them or they don't get the benefits and value of the product. Value added services, on the other hand, must be proactively marketed and sold. Essential services don't need marketing. Solutions not only need marketing, they need a marketing strategy and exceptional selling skills to demonstrate the unique added value.

Some businesses have focused their entire business on solutions. IBM and Capgemini come to mind. How much is a focus on solutions worth? As described in an earlier chapter, firms practicing value based PS pricing in the 2011 Market Rates Study reported PS profitability that is twice as high as those that practice market based PS pricing.

The Legend of Philippe

On his first day as the newly hired plant manager, Jackson Stilson watched in horror as the assembly line ground to a halt. This would cost the company $200,000 per hour. The team on the floor seemed perplexed. He called in a foreman, veteran of 20 years, to learn more. The foreman had two simple words: Call Philippe.

So word went out and soon thereafter a debonair gentleman walked in, asked a couple of questions in a heavy French accent, and immediately walked to machine number 3. He stood on a ladder and turned a set screw. He motioned the foreman to switch on the line and it started without incident. He then shook the foreman's hand and left as quickly as he arrived.

The following day, the invoice arrived for the plant manager's signature. He opened it and stood aghast at a bill for $10,000. He sent the bill back to Philippe, and asked for an itemization. Two days later, the itemized bill arrived. It read: $5 for the time it took to turn the screw. $9,995 for knowing which screw to turn.

TECHNOLOGY SERVICES IN THE MATRIX

In the section above we referenced each cell in the TS Pricing Strategy Matrix and described the services to be found in each. We have expanded the matrix below to include those services. Looking at where services lie in the matrix provides great insight into the challenges of technology services pricing and strategic opportunities for managing those challenges.

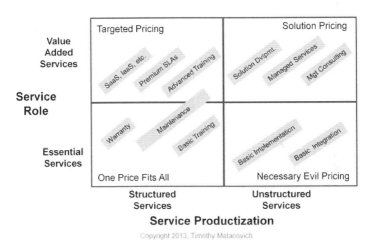

Adding services to the matrix leads to a couple of unavoidable conclusions. First, services fit rather neatly into the 4 quadrants. There is little overlap. Second, service organizations are already offering an abundant array of value added services. Unfortunately, because most use cost based or market based pricing, they are not capturing value based prices. That means they don't sufficiently understand the business impact of their services on a customer's

149

business. They have not designed their offerings to optimize that business impact. And without value understanding and offering design, it is difficult to justify a value based price.

Now take some Nodoz, do 20 pushups. C'mon you can do it. Wake up, because this is a key point. The difference between essential services and value added services is not a distinction between existing services and new to the world services. It is a decision your management team makes about how to package and price services.[25] Let's look at maintenance to illustrate.

Maintenance prices are under pressure. There may be a number of defensive actions a firm can take. One of those is to look closely at the services included in maintenance. The management team should ask: Are there some services in the maintenance pile that are of particular value to some customers and not others? If the answer is yes, then in the graphic above the maintenance label would cross the ES/VAS line. Some services in the maintenance pile are essential services and others are value added services. These value added services are candidates for removal from the pile and Target Pricing. By removing them, we can lower our prices and our cost to serve for the majority of our customers, One Price Fits All, while maintaining margins. For the target customers who truly value these services, they can either remain a part of a "full maintenance" package, or they can be pulled out of maintenance entirely, and repackaged with a higher value price for the target customers who value them.

---

[25] Did you notice I snuck this in and forced you to read it a 4th time?

This leads to a more general lesson to be learned from the matrix. The pricing approach and objectives in each quadrant are distinctly different. To the degree services overlap boundaries, there will be pricing problems. Let's use integration services to illustrate the point. There may be a basic level of proserve necessary to achieve a minimum acceptable level of integration. This may be priced T&M because each integration is somewhat different. Let's say there is an advanced level of integration that you recommend to the customer that may yield 5X the business impact, and it will only require 2X the effort of your team. You would like to price that incremental integration at higher rates than your basic integration, but that is problematic. Not the least of your worries are revenue recognition and VSOE issues.

When I was VP of Strategic Pricing inside a software company, I looked at my relationship with the financial compliance officer as two primary tasks. The first was to assure that we were always in compliance, period. End of report. The second, was to understand VSOE requirements well enough to creatively live within those rules. This is where drawing the big fat red line in the Matrix is important. The line divides essential PS from value added services PS. Willingness to pay is much higher for the latter than the former. Unless you price discriminate between the two, your price capture will always be limited by essential services rates and the Necessary Evil price sensitivity associated with them. In this case, for example, the solution is two teams with different skills and job titles. You need your base integration team and your advanced team, each priced at a different level. VSOE is then established for each. In a T&M world that means you have multiple rate cards.

Rev Rec Advice from the World's Greatest Illusionist
Criss Angel

"I think of myself as a ninja in every area of my life. I am laser focused on achieving my goals. If doors are closed, I figure out how to swing opportunities wide open – whether I have to climb through a window or come out a vent. There's always a way in if you want it bad enough. It's a matter of analyzing, being methodical and putting forth the effort time and commitment to make them happen."

Matrix Moves

The maintenance and integration services examples illustrate matrix moves. Given the market forces at play in technology services, there is a natural movement through the Pricing Strategy Matrix.

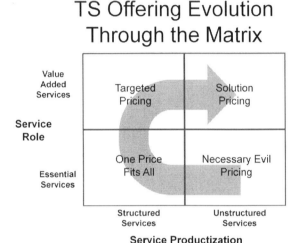

TS Offering Evolution Through the Matrix

Starting again with Necessary Evil Pricing, the pressure on implementation and integration revenues is likely to continue. The solution is to improve efficiency by streamlining and packaging implementation and integration services, to shift them left and up. Move from unstructured implementation to structured implementation. This is exactly what SaaS providers have done to the extent possible with implementation and integration services. Each creates the opportunity for delivering higher value services at lower costs, enabling more profitable growth. If there is an opportunity to package intellectual property to create value added services, so much the better. If you can profitably deliver solutions using your PS team, better still.

One Price Fits All pricing is, as its name implies, ubiquitous. It is less a distinct service price than an extension of the product price. Every product we buy comes with at the very least an implied warranty. In many cases, like basic training, the price may be free. In others, as in maintenance, the price level is high. Whatever the case, the general rule is pull costs out, and don't add any more services to the pile than you absolutely have to. If you need to add services, especially highly valuable services, head north and create value added services with targeted pricing. In most cases, doing this will generate higher margins than adding these services to the pile.

But don't just take my word for it. Maintenance has proven to be a durable money maker for a long time. Margins are enormous. My recommendation is that you do a value pricing analysis every time you consider adding a service to the maintenance pile. If the value is sufficiently high for the service, then keep it out of the pile and make it a distinct offering. If the analysis suggests the highest return is by putting it in the pile, do that. In sum, don't take my word for it. Follow Bill Clinton's advice at the 2012 Democratic convention: Do the arithmetic!

Targeted pricing is where future money is to be made in technology services. Packaging services lowers their costs. Targeting these services to deliver unique value to customer segments increases value delivered and price capture potential. These are services that are unique to your firm, and bundled to create unique value for well defined customers. This is where higher margins are not only possible, but probable.

Finally, Solution Pricing. This is where the firm not only gets paid for its packaged services, but also for its expertise in solving the customer's business problems.

SERVICES STRATEGY AND THE MATRIX

In the chapter on objectives, we reviewed the four service strategy profiles. Matrix pricing strategies fit well with these profiles, as illustrated below.

Service Strategy Profiles and the Matrix

If you are a solution provider, then your pricing strategy falls squarely in that quadrant. If you are a product provider, you want to focus on essential services and the two ES quadrants. If you are a product extender, then you will likely be adding structured value added services to your portfolio and require targeted pricing. If you are a systems provider, you will mix and match as necessary to meet the needs of a given customer, so your pricing may include elements from all four quadrants.

"And so from hour to hour we ripe and ripe. And then from hour to hour we rot and rot. And thereby hangs a tale."

- Touchstone, As You Like It, Wm Shakespeare

CHAPTER 7 - PROACTIVE MANAGEMENT

If your goal is to improve financial performance quickly through pricing, you are in the right place. Better execution is typically the fastest path to finding hidden revenues and reaching higher margins. This is the realm of low hanging fruit. This is the $20 bill you find floating in the dryer. This is the "Bank Error in Your Favor" card in Monopoly. No matter what your pricing belief system – cost based, market based or value based - there are pricing execution opportunities to be exploited. This means pricing pays its own way. A good rule of thumb is: improve execution first and then invest part of the proceeds in strategic pricing improvements. Better execution can help any pricer put more money in the company's pocket. Rewards from improved margins through better execution more than make up for the costs associated with getting them.

There's another reason it makes sense to start with execution and back into strategy. Even the best strategy falls apart if not executed well. What good is a value price or a pricing strategy if the value prop is mis-communicated, if sales discounts the value price away during negotiations, or if account managers bypass process controls? So this chapter focuses on execution improvements independent of strategy improvements.

But before my friend George strings me up by the neck until dead, keep in mind one thing: Better execution powered by good pricing strategy is where the real money is. Pricing strategy is the pricing engine. It is the orchard in which the low hanging fruit tree is found, it is the $1M winning lottery ticket you find in the drier, and it is Boardwalk plus Park Place with hotels, just when you need them most in Monopoly.

UNDERSTANDING PRICING EXECUTION

To understand pricing execution, we must begin with a bit of pricing vocabulary. Virtually everyone has heard that Eskimo's have over a hundred words for snow. As we talk about price, we need to specify what price we are talking about. There are three prices to manage: list price, contract price and pocket price. The exact terms may vary from company to company, so let's describe each to get a shared understating.

- **List Price** is the price that companies decide to ask for their offerings. If you are selling structured services like packaged, fixed fee implementation services or service agreements, then list price is the asking price. If you are a PS organization that prices services T&M, then list prices are the rates on your rate card. If you price maintenance as a percent of the product price, then it is the percent of product price produced by your price calculator. Essentially, the list price is the price you decide for your offering before it is presented to sales.

  Some tech companies use a term like "adjusted list price" to describe list prices after the effects of a policy discount. So, for example, PS adjusted list rates would be rates after a volume discount or a consultant in residency discount is applied. Then they use this adjusted price as their documented list price. The problem is that this leads to a price planning process that never questions the adjustments. My advice is start with a naked list price and then track the adjustments.

- **Contract Price** is the price customers ultimately pay for your offering <u>as it is written on the contract or invoice</u>. This is the price you receive after two types of discounts – policy discounts and discretionary discounts. These discounts combined are also known as "on-invoice" discounts because the effects appear on the invoice. So mathematically,
  - o Contract Price = List Price – (Policy Discounts + Discretionary Discounts)
- **Pocket Price** is the price you actually realize after accounting for items that don't appear on the invoice. For example, if you give away a product to close a sale, that giveaway does not appear on the invoice, but is certainly a price concession. So to determine pocket price you would subtract the price of these "off-invoice" items. Mathematically,
  - o Pocket Price = Contract Price – Off-Invoice Items

Now let's use our old friend the Value-Price Surfboard to illustrate the domain of pricing execution.

Pricing Strategy vs. Pricing Execution

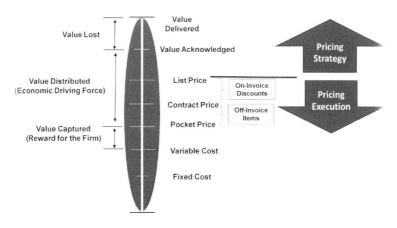

We have sliced the price element of our surfboard into three prices – a list price, a contract price and a pocket price. In my experience the simplest way to think of pricing strategy is starting at list price and heading north. Pricing strategy is focused on value to the customer. The primary pricing strategy questions are

1. What is the value of our offering, and how does that value vary, customer to customer?

2. How should we design our offering and price menu, given that value and how it varies?

3. What price range should we consider, and what level should we set given the price sensitivity of our customer?

Pricing execution starts at the list price and heads south. Pricing execution takes the value, offering design and pricing as given and asks two different questions

1. How do we proactively manage sales in order to enable their pricing success?
2. What must sales do to be effective at capturing price?

Setting the stage for sales success begins with effective pricing process and control. This is the system, including planning, policies and structure that managers use to exercise pricing power consistent with the strategy. For a firm looking to drive higher margins this year, process and control offer quick win opportunities. For example, just yesterday I was speaking to a services manager about his pricing practices. He explained that his sales people routinely offered opening discounts, i.e. they offered discounts to customers before the customer even had an opportunity to respond to the list price. In boxing parlance, this is known as leading with the chin. This practice is easy to stop and a quick win for any pricing leader.

The second element of proactive management is pricing capability. Have you developed the capabilities of your managers and sales people? Do they have the skills and tools necessary to be effective at pricing? The third element is incentives. For the most part, all of us do what we can to escape pain and gain pleasure. Compensation, recognition and performance assessment all encourage effective pricing behavior.

Ultimately, pricing must be turned over to sales. So what specific skills must sales have to effectively execute good pricing? The first is the ability to price qualify the buyer. This is beyond typical sales qualification, and sets the stage for the pricing approach. Second is managing the customers willingness to pay. Customers are willing to pay to the degree they believe in the value of a service. An important sales role, therefore, is assuring that value is being consistently communicated to customers to drive favorable behavior across different buying situations and different decision makers. Finally sales must have the skills and tools to force customers to trade off value for price concessions.

PROACTIVE MANAGEMENT

I specifically use the term "proactive" to make the point that pricing is not a spectator sport. It astonishes me when I hear that a company has not reviewed their pricing "in years". Is there any other element of strategy that suffers the same abuse? This is particularly onerous because price is one half the revenue equation. The following diagram illustrates the essential elements of good pricing management.

Profitable Technology Services Pricing™

4. Proactive Management

What must managers do to enable sales' pricing success?

Exercise Control	Build Pricing Capability	Incent Behavior
Process / Compliance	Skills / Tools / Structure	Comp'n, Recog'n. / Perform Msmt

Copyright 2012, Timothy Matanovich

EXERCISE CONTROL

A few years ago I evaluated the pricing practices of a large technology business. My assessment prompted me to question their commitment to selling value because sales people were paid solely on revenues. Upon hearing my concerns, the general manager dismissed them, assuring me that their sales people were well trained, and policies for controlling price were in place. In a subsequent meeting with the sales team, however, I heard a different story. "Tim, I appreciate what you are saying about capturing price, but I get paid to sell. I will trade off price any day to close a sale."

I begin with this story to make the point that control should not be confused with incentives. Sure pricing control is important, but sales people will circumvent control if necessary when their incentives prompt them to do so. As mentioned above, sales people are often compensated on revenues or

163

volume. They are happy to give up 5% or 10% in price to close a deal because it means they still get 90% to 95% of their commissions. The margin impact is of little concern.

For a sales force accustomed to pricing flexibility, pricing control may be seen as an impediment to closing deals. The value prop may not be clear. The price itself may not be justified, so sales may see no clear connection between price and value. Finance may hike the price to hit margin targets without adequate consideration of customer impact. Or sales may simply have too much pricing authority. Whatever the case, in order to hit their revenue or volume targets, sales may proactively work to undermine price controls. It is not malicious intent. Rather it is simply in their best interests to do so. In these cases, pricing and sales objectives are at odds. It is not unusual for the head of pricing to become known as the "VP of "No!". Conversely, when control is aligned with incentives, control can be highly effective.

The goal is to align incentives and controls to encourage the right sales behavior.

PROCESS

The first element of control is a formal pricing process that governs pricing behaviors. Elements of the pricing process may vary from one service category to the next. In PS, for example, the process may involve a heavy investment in defining requirements and developing a quote, and price is determined during the sales process. With service agreements, price is set based on a formula. In this case, the price formula is determined in advance of the sale, and simply calculated at the time of the sale. Whatever the case, an effective service pricing process has four stages, as illustrated below.

Essential Pricing Process Stages

Copyright 2013 Timothy Matanovich

Think of the pricing process this way. It is the OtterBox® that defends the firm's profitability. If you have been living in a cave the last few years, OtterBox is the protective plastic and rubber case that you place your stylish smartphone in to protect it from the hazards of day to day existence. The pricing process lays over the firm's marketing and sales processes to assure the interests of profitability are served.

Before we dive into each of these stages in more detail, note that pricing modus operandi in many service organizations largely starts in the third stage – Configure Offerings and Decide Pricing. Little effort is taken during the price planning process or during the early stages of the sales process to evaluate the customers' willingness to pay or to quantify the impact on the customer's business. These organizations set service prices using cost based or market based pricing shortcuts. Missing these first two steps sets the stage for weak communication of value and price concessions instead of value-price tradeoffs later in the process.

With essential services, this may not be a bad default decision. The value of essential services is largely subsumed in the product value. Moving to value added services, however, the first steps in the pricing process become vital.

An effective pricing process begins with price qualifying the buyer. In the broadest sense, price qualification includes providing sales with target markets and prospects to pursue. It is not unusual in most sales processes for sales to qualify the customer to determine that she has budget to work with, and that the company's offerings can meet her needs. Price qualifying goes beyond that to ask, for example, is this a price buyer or a value buyer? In other words, is this prospect looking for the lowest price service that will meet her well defined needs, or is she looking for a service package that drives an important KPI? The answer to this question defines the competitive set and informs sales about what kinds of offers, communications and negotiation strategies are likely to be successful. Price qualification sets the stage for the rest of the pricing process.

My favorite sales book is *Let's Get Real or Let's Not Play.*[26] Three principles are central to their thesis.

1. World class solutions require world class inquiry.
2. Business impact must be quantified
3. Focus on the customer's high priority business problems first.

---

[26] Mahan Khalsa and Randy Illig, Let's Get Real or Let's Not Play – Transforming the Buyer/Seller Relationship

Maybe you need a full blown business case with a 3 year NPV analysis to justify customer's investment. Maybe it is working through the financial consequences of their business problem on the back of an envelope. Maybe it is services management quantifying value to a target segment of customers. The important point is that somewhere along the line, someone has assessed the business impact with some degree of rigor. And that impact can be well communicated during the sales process.

Considering the qualification of the buyer and the impact your services will have on their value drivers, an offer and price menu need to be developed. Offering and price menu development were covered in the chapter on pricing design. The goal of good offering design is that it permits sales to recommend discrete options with real value differences, and sets the stage for value tradeoffs.

A value driven communication plan is then developed, as well as a negotiating plan. The communication plan is an integrated effort by marketing and sales to demonstrate and document the value delivered by the services. Demonstrating value is the use of an economic value calculator, spreadsheet to estimate the value of the recommended service solution. Documenting value is the use of case evidence that proves value delivery. It is one thing to run an economic model with a client that says he will increase margins by 5%. It is altogether another thing to back that up with cases that support those findings. This is not an overnight fix, but within 12 months it can become a powerful tool in your sales person's arsenal.

The negotiating plan begins with diagnosing buyer behavior and forces customers to trade off options with real value differences in order to get a lower price.

This pricing process should be mapped out, and include the following elements.

1. Who has authority, what authority they have and under what conditions that authority is granted.
2. Information required to request a price quote or adjustment
3. Outputs from the pricing process, including not only the quote but sales comp implications

Aside from increasing margins, increasing clarity and confidence in prices will lead to other benefits as well. When sales people know the rules, they gain negotiating power. Moreover, less management time is lost in endless debates about price. With less debate around price, deals close faster. Faster closing accelerates turnover, increasing revenues again.

COMPLIANCE

Compliance might be thought of in two components: policies and enforcement. The pricing process itself is a set of policies governing pricing behavior. The price menu is the set of policies that governs what prices can be offered for what. Finally, there is the set of policies that govern pricing authority and limits on that authority. Following is an example of these Pricing Authority Controls.

Pricing Authority Control

Decision Authority	Sales Management	SVP Business Unit	COO/CFO
Negotiation Limits			
E.g. New Perpetual or Term License (Discretionary Discounts from Adjusted List Price)	Up to 8%	Up to 14%	Above 14%
Reporting from Sales (Required for revised quote)	Price Adjustment Request form	⟶	
Pricing Tools (Decision making aids for sales and product management.	Quote & Compensation Report	1.Monthly Price Performance Reports, including a win-loss analysis specifying the cost of lost deals 2.Bi-weekly Discount Report	
Quote Production, Process Oversight & Compliance Monitoring	Pricing Operations		
Executive Oversight	SVP Sales	EVP Product Management	
Rewards & Consequences	Sales Compensation	Performance Review	

Pricing authority controls should specify three things. Who has authority, what authority they have and under what conditions that authority may be exercised. Note the example above also includes a description of who is responsible for oversight and specifies rewards and consequences.

Because monitoring pricing compliance can sometimes be as slippery as a baby in a bathtub, and as elusive as a two-year old with ADD, I recommend establishment of a Pricing Review Authority to monitor compliance. The specific charter will vary from company to company, but monitoring compliance and establishing enforcement mechanisms should be a central role. Compliance oversight should focus on answering three questions.

1. Is the documented pricing process being lived day to day by the organization?

2. Is the pricing menu being adhered to?

169

3.   Are pricing authority controls complied with?

In a subsequent chapter, I discuss price performance measurement.   That chapter includes suggested tools for monitoring compliance.   Needless to say, 100% compliance is an unachievable goal.   Here the Pareto Principle applies. Do we have compliance in the 20% of cases governing 80% of our revenues?

BUILD PRICING CAPABILITIES

Many product sales people dislike selling services.   Service sales frequently involve complex developments that evolve over longer sales cycles.   In many technology firms, product sales people actively discourage PS sales activities, especially early in the sales cycle[27].   Research study after research study conducted by TSIA report the same findings: Selling services requires different skills than selling products.   Further, firms who have a dedicated services sales motion discount less and earn higher services margins than those that don't.

Beyond this high level, the role of service sales in pricing success varies dramatically based on the strategy outlined in the pricing strategy matrix.   In the case of solution pricing, an important role of service sales is to discover the value of solving a business problem in order to drive offering design and pricing.   Here value analysis is a critical skill for sales.   In the case of a One Price Fits All, maintenance pricing, service design and price are already established. Here the role of services sales is relegated in most cases to the product sales team.

---

[27] In the 2009 PSA Market Rates Study, nearly 2/3 of global technology firms reported this kind of behavior.

SKILLS

Beyond the pricing strategy, required sales skills will also differ based on the service offering itself. The following table uses professional services as an example of how sales capabilities vary depending on whether services are sold in a staffing model or project model.

What skill sets are required?

Sales Skill	Staffing Sales	Project Sales
Product Knowledge	Deep but not broad	Broad but not deep
Business Knowledge	Limited	Extensive
Situation Diagnosis	Staff skills match only	Customer business analysis
Relationship Building	Limited	Extensive
Value Communication	Staff skills related	Solution/System related
Competitive Knowledge	People focused	Solution focused

If you are in the staffing business, then the skills you need are the ability to match available resources to client requirements. If you are in the project business, then you need a deeper set of skills. In this case the management team must recruit and develop sales staff that have three unique skills:

- **Diagnostic** – Successful project sales professionals develop excellent diagnostic skills. Frequently this starts with the ability to ask penetrating questions and includes superior "listening" skills. Successful sales personnel learn to ask precipitating questions that get at not just the "presenting symptoms" of client problems, but the underlying systemic issues that are the heart of successful project interventions. Probing questions are critical in this regard. As the sales staff builds an understanding of the underlying, systemic issues, they must then be skilled at assessing appropriate service offering components. These skills can be refined as sales staff participate not only in the selling effort, but also in the delivery effort for selected projects.

- **Negotiation** – Successful project sales staff develop expertise in diagnosing client buying behavior; some clients buy strictly on price (low price is critical), others buy on delivered value, while still others are relationship buyers. The negotiating process varies based on the client's underlying buying behavior. And, the appropriate service offering menu varies on the basis of that behavior. Finally, successful sales personnel refuse to negotiate price; instead, they focus their negotiation on forcing clients to trade offering elements that decrease value delivery in exchange for lower prices – forcing clients to sacrifice value delivery if they insist on price concessions.

- **Communication** – Achieving value based prices requires sales staff to invest considerable effort in communicating value delivery and managing the emotive factors that affect client price sensitivity. Successful sales professionals spend more time understanding the client's business and communicating value impact than talking about their services.

The implications of available selling skills can be significant for price achievement. If you price projects with a staffing mindset, you end up leaving a lot of money on the table. In virtually every case the value of the project is greater than the value of the individual team members who deliver the project. If you price staffing with a project mindset, you are likely to overprice engagements and lose sales because what the customer really wants to buy is a well defined set of skills that he can use to create value.

Bottom line for management is that you need to develop the pricing capabilities of your people. The capabilities you require vary depending largely on the kinds of pricing you do. You can utilize the TS Pricing Strategy Matrix to begin the determination of your needs. Structured services require product management and marketing skills to design offerings and construct price menus. Unstructured services require more skilled sales people with the ability to communicate and negotiate. Essential services require more market based pricing skills. Value added services require value based pricing skills.

TOOLS

This book is filled with tools for pricing. Let's take a moment to focus on sales. What kinds of tools might sales need to be effective at pricing

Capability	Tools
Targeting and Price Qualifying the Buyer	Buyer Profile Worksheet
Increase Willingness to pay	Value proposition and presentation Process for demonstrating value Cases documenting value EVS Calculator Price sensitivity tool
Buying Process Management	Matrix for mapping value drivers to decision makers Action plans for selling value across the buying center

Force Value Tradeoffs	Offering Options
	Price Menu
	Tradeoff tool describing value and cost
	implications of tradeoffs.

Use of tools also call for rules of engagement. For example Baldor Corporation produces a marvelous, customizable value calculator that can calculate total cost of ownership.[28] It has made companies who use it hundreds of millions of dollars. Baldor recommends, however, that the tool be used only in 10% to 20% of sales engagements, where the investment required to use the tool is amply paid for by the return on sales performance.

STRUCTURE

Continuing the example above, what happens if you have the same sales people selling staffing and project work? This is the case with many tech firms. The answer can be found with physics. The principle of entropy applies in pricing. Entropy is the directionality in the universe. You can knock a glass off a table and break it, but you will never see a broken glass arise from the floor and reassemble itself on the table (except in the movies). Similarly if the same sales people sell staffing and project work, everything will tend to sell at the lower staffing price. At least some of the project value will be lost and project prices will tend to fall to the lowest price – the staffing price. Pricing entropy is the fact that prices naturally fall to the lowest possible level unless fences are built that prevent them from doing so.

---

[28] Baldor TCO Toolbox www.baldor.com

So how can the firm use sales structure to better defend prices? The solution might be found in using "buyer triage". Let's say one of your project consultants is asked for a staffing quote. Instead of providing it, they forward the request to the staffing sales center. Since staffing requests are fairly straightforward, they can be handled by a staffing sales person who has staff availability information at their fingertips. A quote can be quickly provided to the customer. Since the cost of sales is lower, the firm can sell staffing at a lower price and still have a higher margin.

This frees up the project managers time to sell more project engagements where their skills are needed. In addition, because they are not dealing with low price staffing sales, they are better mentally prepared to sell value and capture a value based price. A project price could be distinguished from the staffing price in a number of ways: fixed bid vs. T&M, different job titles, different rate card, solution swat teams, etc.

What's the potential payback of buyer triage? In one case we worked, buyer triage resulted in an 8% increase in revenues and a whopping 111% increase in service business profitability. It's the classic case of the difference between doing things right and doing the right thing. Doing the right thing in this case resulted in a handsome payback.

Note how the pieces of the sales puzzle fit together. Capturing higher prices requires effective communication of value, effective communication requires sales people with the right skills, sales structure permits the firm to triage buyers, permitting sales work to be allocated to those best suited to the task, and finally pricing policies permit different prices to be charged for staffing and project engagement.

INCENT BEHAVIOR

When it comes to pricing execution, the single greatest challenge facing technology services managers is sales incentives. In too many cases, the incentives of the sales organization are misaligned with the objectives of the business. Experience has shown that if sales incentives are not tied in a significant way to margin or a proxy, like price, then sales people will be strongly inclined to discount services to close a deal. The following case illustrates the problem and path to a solution.

I was meeting with the president of a middle market software company. He said "the reason we need your help is profitability. We have grown a $160M business, but our profitability is virtually zero." My response was "the fastest thing you can do is change sales incentives. Do that, and we can turn around profitability next year." We made that change, and had double digit profits the next year. Perhaps the most interesting part of the story is what happened to service prices. The incentive program was applied across the board – products and services – with equivalent force. To our surprise, the greatest impact was on service prices. Perhaps the sales force recognized that service prices had more potential upside (were more inelastic) than product prices. We saw the change in both professional and managed services.

In my view, sales compensation is the acid test of effective execution. As a friend of mine at Penn State is fond of saying: "Good sales people are coin operated." Given that reality, sales people will in most cases use price discounts to close a deal unless they are paid to do otherwise. The following exhibit illustrates the problem and the solution.

Revenue + Price Based Commissions

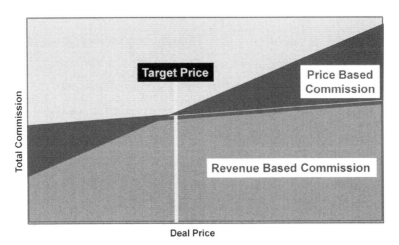

Copyright 2013. Timothy Matanovich

The dark blue line represents the typical revenue based commission on a deal. The lower axis of the graph is deal price. If sales people are paid simply on revenues, then they are happy to give up 1% or 5% of the deal price because they are still getting 99% or 95%, respectively, of their full commission. Unfortunately, since a 1% change in price can translate into a 10% change in operating profit, the margin impact is -10% or -50% respectively!

One system to solving the problem is to add a price based commission on top of the revenue based commission, the dark red line. If sales closes the deal at a price higher than the target, then they are rewarded handsomely for their price performance. If they close the deal at a price lower than the target, then their commission is likewise painfully reduced. This compensation puts marketing, finance and sales all on the same page, focused on profitability instead of just revenues. It is the single most effective technique for improving sales pricing performance.

As a practical matter, I often get questions about how much of sales comp should be dedicated to profit or price target achievement. Let's start by saying different sales organizations construct compensation in different ways. Some relay heavily on fixed compensation. Others rely heavily on variable comp. For pricing incentives purposes, work with variable comp. In my experience the profit or price target element of compensation should be at minimum 30% of variable comp. Every case I have seen where it is less has turned out to be ineffective. 30% seems to be the minimum to get sales attention. On the high side, I think 50% is the right number. Again, I have seen firms set variable comp 100% based on profit. In my experience, this kind of compensation does not deliver the growth that most tech companies want. The goal of technology services pricing in most cases is profitable growth. As a result, I recommend setting the price/profit component of variable comp at 50%. If you get pushback, set it at 30%. Below 30% you are wasting your time.

It is worth mentioning I have also seen organizations make the change and see no change in sales behavior. This scenario suggests two remedies. First, you need to do the marketing. In one case, as part of the quoting process, we estimated the impact on the sales person's compensation. If they requested a lower price they immediately saw the impact on their comp. That is, sales got real time feedback on the link between price and comp on every single deal; every single re-quote. Second, the issue may be capabilities. In one of the Mad Max movies, Max is tied to a donkey and left in the desert. The donkey has a bottle of water attached to a stick that hangs in front of its nose. The donkey will walk forever to reach that water, but is doomed to failure. Sales people need the skills and tools to actually achieve what the incentive is driving them to do.

Implementing this change in compensation will also result in other changes in sales behavior. Sales will hunt down more profitable customers and work proactively to sell value. They will pressure the organization to improve product and service quality and get clearer on competitor strengths and weaknesses. Finally, sales will demand training, since training helps them sell value. In turn, selling value that commands higher prices means higher commissions.

Beyond monetary incentives there are recognition and performance review. Everybody wants an ataboy or an atagirl. When I headed up pricing inside of a company, annually I recognized product management and sales people with the "1% award" for pricing excellence. These awards were constant reminders to keep price in mind in business decision making. At sales meetings, revenues are often recognized. What about margin? Make delivered margin a recognition point at sales events.

Recognizing and rewarding pricing excellence in performance reviews can help busy people keep price and margin priorities at the top of their agendas.

"You do not pay the price of success, you enjoy the price of success"

- Zig Ziglar

CHAPTER 8 - SALES EFFECTIVENESS

All the strategy and management in the world is useless unless sales makes your price a reality with customers, one at a time. Early in this book we discussed the context for pricing and its central tenet.

Manage the Value Exchange
Create and sustain a business environment in which sales and customers are forced to acknowledge and pay for service value delivery.

The key to sales effectiveness is for sales people to create and sustain an environment where customers are forced to acknowledge and pay for service value delivery. This involves two pieces of work within the sales process: price qualifying the buyer, and then based on that buyer profile, managing that buyer's willingness to pay.

A popular misconception is that pricing and sales are inherently at odds. In fact, the opposite is true. Good pricing practices enhance sales capabilities and effectiveness. Better pricing increases negotiating power, shortens the sales cycle and rewards sales for capturing more profitable revenues. So good pricing is anything but in the way of the sale. Our objective here is not only to close the sale, but to do it fairly – for the customer and for the firm. The goal is win-win.

The following graphic illustrates the key skills that sales needs to be effective at capturing price.

Profitable Technology Services Pricing[TM]

5. Sales Effectiveness

What must sales do to be effective at capturing price?

Price Qualify the Buyer	Manage Willingness to Pay
• Target Value Buyers • Diagnose Buyer Behavior • Classify the Buy Situation	• Present the Value and Price • Manage the Buying Process • Negotiate Tradeoffs

Copyright 2013 Timothy Matanovich

PRICE QUALIFY THE BUYER

I've said it earlier and I will say it again: "Not all buyers are created equal." Some customers are simply willing to pay more than others. Some customers cost more to serve than others. Some customers value the unique characteristics of our offerings, while others do not. Some will demand the lowest price and you know you will lose the sale if you don't deliver. Others want the relationship with you and your firm and pay your price without question. The sales person needs to sort through these options so he can decide how best to present the price and negotiate the sale.

TARGET VALUE BUYERS

In the sections on strategy we repeatedly stressed the importance of targeting the right customers. If sales are to consistently succeed at capturing value through price, then they need to be selling to customers who value the differentiation of your offering. This is the job of marketing and sales management, to direct sales people toward the most valuable prospects. Targeting the right companies and buyers is the first task of price qualifying the buyer.

Probably the most money I have ever made for a company was the result of good targeting. A multi-national telecomm firm was trying to establish a beach head in the American market. They called my firm after losing three deals in a row valued at over $200M. Price discounting had won them nothing. A segmentation analysis revealed they were targeting segments where the competitor was King Kong compared to their Cheetah (i.e. Tarzan's sidekick). The recommendation of the analysis was a no brainer: target the segments where you are relatively strong compared to the big gorilla. Taking our recommendations to heart, our client redirected their efforts and closed 3 of the next 4 deals, all in segments where they had competitive advantage. They were successful at their list price.

Diving one level deeper, who to target within an account is in transition. Historically IT sellers sold ultimately to the CIO or CTO. Today functional buyers are playing a greater role. In most cases, these functional buyers are the keys to both understanding and selling value added services into the organization.

DIAGNOSE BUYER BEHAVIOR

The second element of the work is actually price qualifying the buyer as part of the selling process. Price qualification can be diagnosed by asking and answering two basic questions.

1. How much does this customer care about service differentiation?
2. How much does this customer care about service price?

The first question relates to the unique characteristics of our service offering as compared to competitive alternatives. Does your customer believe that your offering is meaningfully different than the competition and that those differences matter to his business success? Some customers care a lot about the differences. Some customers care little. For example some customers would never think of outsourcing services to a third party. Others rely on third parties because they get the same value as employees without all the administration. In fact, some firms use employee leasing for exactly this reason.

The second question is about price. Some customers care a lot about price, others don't. A Colorado manufacturer nearly went out of business during the early 2000s when their customers moved their orders to China. The firm was just one more casualty of "the China price". A year later a dock worker strike in Los Angeles disrupted shipments, and those same customers came back to the Colorado firm asking it to fulfill orders until the strike was resolved. The manager was happy to oblige – at ten times its historic price. Customers happily paid because the cost of the disruption far exceeded the cost of the parts. He subsequently built a highly profitable business of meeting customers' short term needs.

The answers to the questions about differentiation and price sensitivity enable us to construct a simple model to diagnose customer behaviors and develop tactics for dealing with them.[29]

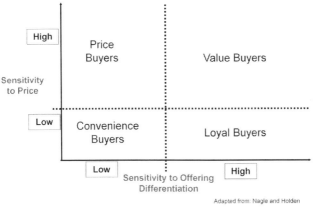

Four Classic Buyer Behaviors

1. **Price Buyers.** Every sales person knows a price buyer. To hear some sales people tell it, they are all price buyers. The first part of their mantra is "We want your lowest price". The second part of their mantra is "and our requirements are minimal". It is important to be cognizant of both parts of this mantra. These are organizations that will consider all service suppliers that meet their minimum requirements, and may choose to use multiple providers if the opportunity presents itself. They really don't make price – value tradeoffs, but buy on price alone. The simple fact is that they don't

_____

[29] Thomas Nagle and Reed Holden, The Strategy and Tactics of Pricing

care about your differentiation. They will limit your access to decision makers who might introduce any consideration other than price into the mix. Finally they may very well pit competing suppliers against one another to get the best price.

2. **Value Buyers.** These are sophisticated, thoughtful buyers that are willing to pay more for higher value offerings if forced to do so. Their mantra: "We want your value at a competitive price." They will consider multiple suppliers, if that option is available, and will trade off price for value. Price is important to them, and they may negotiate aggressively with potential suppliers, but they definitely have an eye on the upside potential. Since they are focused on value and willing to trade, they will switch suppliers if it is in their best interest to do so.

3. **Relationship Buyers.** Every sales person also knows a relationship buyer or two. Their Mantra: "We want a solid solution from a supplier we trust". For these buyers, value takes precedence over price. More specifically, relationship value trumps both offering value and price. These buyers are either loyal to you or loyal to a competitor. If they are loyal to you, they generally won't give other suppliers more than lip service. They perceive the costs of switching suppliers to be high, whether costs are in fact high or not. Finally they typically don't haggle over price.

4. **Convenience Buyers.** To paraphrase Queen, these buyers want it all and want it now. They often choose the first offering that comes along, and buy based on availability. They don't invest a lot of time researching alternatives. Like relationship buyers, they don't typically haggle over price.

Reading this it may occur to you that there may be a correlation between buyer types and pricing strategies as described in the TS Pricing Strategy Matrix.

Indeed there are, but the truth is you may run into any buyer type in any situation. That said, here are some likelihoods.

1. You are likely to encounter price buyers when you are employing a One Price Fits All strategy or a Necessary Evil Pricing strategy for essential services.

2. You are likely to encounter value buyers or relationship buyers when you are using a Targeted Pricing strategy for value added, structured services.

3. You are likely to encounter relationship buyers when you are using a Solution Pricing strategy and selling value added, unstructured services.

I get a couple of questions routinely when I talk through these buyer types with clients. The first question is whether these buyer types represent organizations of individuals. My experience is that they represent the culture of the organization, though any individual may vary. Note that the same buyer may behave differently depending on the purchase. If a buyer needs support for software instrumental to their operational success, they may behave like a value buyer: paying a premium price for your premium support. If they are looking for support for some old, but serviceable hardware, they might look for the lowest price, period. Also, procurement is trained to behave like a price buyer, whether the actual buyer is or is not.

The second question I often get is about how many companies fall into each quadrant. Note the dashed lines in my chart above. This is somewhat indicative of the relative size of the groups. Convenience buyers are typically the smallest group. Customers have urgent needs, but they are not every customer and not daily occurrences. Price buyers are often assumed to be more numerous than they actually are. This is especially true in services. How many customers actually want a commodity level of service at the lowest price? Not many. In fact, I recently worked with a company where 80% of their customers subscribed to their highest level of service. Regarding relationship buyers, I am not sure. I could well subscribe to the argument that services are a relationship business. As a result, a higher portion of service buyers are relationship buyers.

Finally, value buyers comprise the largest group. This is especially true in services. I can hear it now – all of you nattering nabobs of negativism are going to tell me that value buyers are a vanishing breed. It is more and more about price. For those of you willing to stuff a sock in your piehole for a few minutes, I suggest you consider this. It is not that value buyers are becoming fewer. Rather it is that value buyers find they can get a better price for value received by pretending to be price buyers and employ aggressive negotiating tactics. This is where your ability to diagnose becomes very important indeed.

To manage price well, each type of buyer should be treated differently. A winning process is to identify the type of buyer and then to develop your proposal and negotiating strategy accordingly. The qualification stage in the sales process should include questions on price qualifying the buyer. Here is a sampling of some useful diagnostic questions.

Questions	Typical Answers			
Buyer Type	Value Buyers	Price Buyers	Relation'p Buyers	Conven. Buyers
How many service suppliers are being considered?	Few/Many	Many	Few/One	Few/One
How fast do they need to make a decision?	Not Fast	Fast	Not Fast	Fast
How important is your differentiation?	Important	Not Important	Important	Not Important
How many people are involved in the decision?	Many/Few	Few/One	Few/One	Few/One

So let's look at how to manage each type of buyer.

MANAGING PRICE BUYERS

If managed well, price buyers may be both your easiest buyers to manage and your most profitable buyers. The reason? Their needs are well defined and unambiguous: they have minimal requirements and want your lowest price. The biggest risk you face is winning a deal that is either unprofitable or may damage your ability to get profitable business elsewhere, e.g. with another department in the same company.

- Rule number one is to decide in advance when to walk away. Only accept contracts that are profitable in the short run.
- Don't get sucked into a feeding frenzy of a bidding war or price competition.
- Strip offerings to the minimum. These buyers are unwilling to pay for value, so don't deliver beyond the minimum value.
- Meaningfully differentiate your offering to the price buyer, so that she understands it is different from what you would offer a value or relationship buyer.
- If they want services or other add-ons, upcharge for them.
- They don't want a relationship, so don't invest in one.
- Watch out for contracts that commit you but not them.

In some cases, price buyers can be your largest customers, so managed well their cost to serve can be low. These customers can be quite profitable.

VALUE BUYERS

Value buyers want to see improved business performance and are willing to invest to make it happen. They do their homework, consider a number of suppliers and focus on the service value relative to price asked. The risk is that you don't sell value aggressively enough. If they don't respect you for your value they will devolve into price buyers. Think of value buyers as a Hollywood marriage – great when the chemistry is good, but not much of a relationship over time. They don't want the relationship, they want the business impact.

- You must start with absolute confidence in the differential value of your offering.

- Help the buyer make value comparisons. It demonstrates your confidence and understanding.
- Throw in the kitchen sink if it will have a value impact, and creatively structure your offering to meet their needs
- Be ready to unbundle services in response to price pressure. Always ask for a tradeoff when granting a price concession.
- Be extra careful of gainshare or price for performance requests.

If your services are truly differentiating, then value buyers can be very profitable customers.

RELATIONSHIP BUYERS

Relationship buyers believe in the relationship and service benefits that may accrue, more than in the value of an individual offering. They expect you to take care of them. Golf days and ski days are welcome. Functional value of the offering and price are secondary considerations.

- Demonstrate empathy with their situation, work cooperatively to find solutions
- Offer complete solutions, and don't force them to shop the competition.
- Invest in the relationship and don't exploit it.
- Demonstrate your commitment to their success.

If they are loyal to competitors, avoid being used to complete the file. In other words don't waste your time only to become column fodder. Pursue them only if you have a powerful offering that can overcome high relationship inertia or you have some clear indication they are ready to change suppliers. You can waste a lot of time and never sell anything to a relationship buyer.

191

CONVENIENCE BUYERS

Convenience buyers want it now. Every dad or mom knows this situation. You have young children at home you haven't seen for days. You are racing through the airport and decide you can't live without the overpriced toy from the airport kiosk. Convenience buyers have an urgent and costly problem, and they are willing to pay a premium for a rapid solution.

- The big risk is pricing too high if they are an existing customer.
- Quickly define and scope their needs. The buyer is typically not fussy.
- Focus the buyer on the cost of the problem.
- Price at a premium for the urgent service value.
- If the urgent need is predictable, i.e. you have a customer that always hits you at the last minute, make it a part of your normal price structure for "rush orders"

If it is an existing customer, proceed with caution. Consider moderating your price premium. If it is a new buyer, it pays to be curious. Why are they coming to you? Is there a possible new customer relationship to be developed?

CLASSIFY THE BUY SITUATION

One of the costliest mistakes in services pricing is the one size fits all approach to pricing. I'm not talking about the one price fits all strategy described earlier. For essential structured services, one size fits all makes sense. Rather I am talking about companies not adjusting prices for different buy situations.

Classic marketing theory describes three buy classes: New Purchase, Modified Re-buy and Straight Re-buy. In TS, there is an added level of complexity. This is the presence or absence of a product. Price sensitivity changes depending on the relationship between the product price and the service price. For example, a customer believes that investment in new marketing software could really transform her business. Now let's say the price of the software is $1M and the implementation is $100K. Her service price sensitivity is low because the implementation cost is only a fraction of product price. In this case, any pushback on price is likely to be on the product rather than the service. Alternatively, let's say the product price is $300K and the implementation is $800K, same total price. Now pushback is going to focus more strongly on the services and less on the product. Perceived value remains the same in each case, but the price sensitivity changes depending on the buy situation.

In the absence of a product, managers typically find willingness to pay for services higher. Several factors might explain this willingness to pay.

- Service prices are inherently less price elastic than product prices
- Service value is front and center at the time of a service only sale
- Services sold alone are often sold by service sales specialists.
- Service sales at the time of the product sale are ES, whereas services sold alone are VAS

In sum, it makes sense to consider what buy situation you find yourself in and evaluate willingness to pay from there.

Regarding classic buy situations, the marketing director purchaser described above is a New Purchase. Customers are looking for a solution and the value of that solution is at the front of their minds. In general, price sensitivity is lowest at the time of the initial purchase. Your service sale is part of a larger product + service sale. The question is: How do you convincingly demonstrate your value delivery to affirm their decision to choose you? This may involve case studies and customer references. Your business model determines whether service or product plays the lead role. The role of services and the relative size of the service buy determine the degree of services price sensitivity.

Maintenance renewal is a classic case of a Straight Re-Buy. Simply put, you want customers to renew their maintenance agreements. Since maintenance is largely a warranty that guarantees a certain level of performance over time, the price is largely based on the continuing delivery of the product value. As a pricer, your goal is to demonstrate and document continuing value delivery. The best way to do that is to leverage information you have about the performance of your offering in the customer's own business. Ordinarily a re-buy is the most price sensitive buy situation because it is tough to make the value case when your solution works. What do you compare it to? Fortunately in the world of software, it is often difficult for a third party to provide maintenance services. So some tech companies have a powerful lever to hold the line on maintenance prices. With hardware, however, third party competitors are more common. As a result, hardware maintenance and support is often priced at a fraction of the price of comparable software maintenance. With the increasing role of software in tech products, it remains to be seen if companies will be able to leverage software value and its proprietary nature to increase prices – whether that value capture is within the product itself or through services.

The third case is a Modified Re-Buy. In these cases the customer's service needs have changed. An important part of qualifying the buyer, then, is to discover whether new service needs have emerged since the last renewal. In other words, is it a straight re-buy or a modified re-buy. If customer needs have changed, then it creates an opportunity for upsell at the time of renewal. From a pricing perspective, there are a few key questions to ask

- How important are these new needs?
- Will solving them have a meaningful impact on the customer's business?
- How does the sales process change as a result of this discovery?

This last question is key. If there are indeed meaningful new needs, then the sales process begins anew. There are new value and new benefits to sell. This is the justification for capturing a new price – hopefully higher. Frankly, it may also be that needs have shifted lower. Then the challenge is to maintain the profitability of the relationship even if revenues may fall.

MANAGE WILLINGNESS TO PAY

As pricers in a B2B technology services sales process, what are we trying to accomplish? The answer is we are trying to increase the customer's willingness to pay for value delivered. This includes presenting the value and price, managing the buying process and negotiating tradeoffs of value in exchange when the customer pushes for a lower price.

PRESENT THE VALUE AND PRICE

When we present the offer to the customer, we are setting the stage for our pricing. In fact, you could argue that your entire sales and marketing effort and everything we have discussed so far in this book sets the stage for this moment. Now everything is in the hands of the sales director. His first job is to present the value of the offering and its price.

Let's start by putting this in the context of the 4 buyer types described above. If you are pitching to a price buyer, then your message is that you are the best choice because you have a low price and you can deliver on his minimal requirements. If the pitch is to a value buyer, it is that your offering has unique characteristics that will powerfully impact their business. If you are selling to a convenience buyer, your claim is that you can meet their requirements fast. Finally, if you are selling to a relationship buyer, it is that you are their best partner for life. So your presentation of value begins with that understanding.

Then we need to come back to a fundamental understanding of value, i.e. that value is built on differentiation. Value is relative. In other words your offering has value compared to the customer doing it themselves, or compared to them using another service package in your portfolio or compared to them engaging a third party service provider. Your value is always presented in the context of their next best alternative. Why? Because customers always have options. They don't have to choose you. They don't have to pay your price.

This is differential value. Focus on the handful of reasons your offering is different, and don't waste a lot of time on the 92 reasons it is exactly the same. Actually, focus on the 2 or 3 things that put money in the customer's pocket and forget the rest. You want to make the case for the 2-3 differentiating attributes that have business impact – that is BI (business impact) not BS.

The reference will change depending on the buy situation. In a new product sale, where services are part of the deal, the reference value is the whole product + service offering. That is what customers are comparing. In these cases, the service sale is largely an extension of the product sale. In this case the differentiation is likely against your primary product competitor or against the customer doing it themselves.

On the other hand, if the customers bought and installed your software product 3 years ago, the game has changed. There are perhaps different decision makers and a different business climate. The customer may be a captive customer, so his choices may be between your service levels rather than yours versus the competition. Your reference may be your other offering options. The question the customer needs to answer is: Given his business situation today, which of your service offerings gives him the best ROI? Then he can decide on which to choose and how much to pay.

In other cases you may be facing third party service organizations, but the customer is totally loyal. They would not switch unless their life depended on it. Again, the third party prices may be largely irrelevant. My point in each of these cases is to realistically frame the competitive set.

I mentioned earlier that my favorite sales book is titled *Let's Get Real or Let's Not Play* by Mahan Khalsa. You have to admit, the title itself is great. So let's get real with pricing.

1. You start with the reference value. In many cases, that is going to be your current level of service. You elaborate how much they pay and what they get (the value and benefits). Do they agree? If yes, move on.

2. If you have done your sales homework, you are ready to recommend a future plan. Let's say you think they would benefit from a higher level service offering. The second step is to make the case for the expanded service, relative to their current plan, and why the value to them is greater. Do they agree? If yes, move on.

3. Advise them of any negative consequences of the move and how to mitigate them. Let's say an element of their current plan that is important to them, is missing from the higher level plan. Proactively tell them and give them a path to resolution. Perhaps your higher level plan manages

the customer's issue in a different way. So explain it. Is this going to be a problem? If yes, manage it.

4. Present the price in the context of the incremental value and benefits of the higher level service offering. Here's how your business will be better with the advanced service and here is the price.

Getting real with price is helping the customer make a clear connection between value received and price paid.

Perhaps you are questioning step 3. Do you really want to tell the customer about a potential shortcoming of your offering? What if we have an external competitor? The answer is if the buyer has done his homework, then he is going to be familiar with the advantages and shortcomings of both offerings. Not acknowledging them is disingenuous and a bit ostrich like. [30] Recommendation: Acknowledge them and move on. This will give you credibility with your buyer.

As you are working with your customer, describing value and presenting price, here are a few guidelines to keep in mind

- If the reference you choose has a relatively low price, then customers will be more price sensitive when presented with a high price
- If customer perceives risk in the decision, their sensitivity to price will go up. Hence, special "introductory offers".
- If the customer incurs switching costs moving from one offering to another, then those costs will increase the customer's price sensitivity.

---

[30] James Anderson, Value Merchants, Demonstrating and Documenting Value in Business Markets

The possibility of incurring these costs will also make customers resistant to switch between competitors.

- Your price may be an indicator of your service quality. Higher prices may actually reduce price sensitivity and differentiate you from the competition.

- If the service expenditure is small or relatively small in the total deal, then the buyer is unlikely to be price sensitive. On the other hand, service agreements like maintenance may be the second largest IT expenditure and a target for cost cutters.

- Ultimately will the buyer perceive your price as fair? If not, then their lizard brain starts tingling and makes them more price sensitive.

> ### *My Friend Carl*
> *Carl is an agent of Northwestern Mutual Life and has been my advisor for 20 years or more. He is also one of NML's top agents. Top agent in one of the world's top sales organizations. Every meeting with Carl starts in exactly the same way – "Let's look at how your program is working for you." In other words, Carl was demonstrating his value and establishing a reference point. Then he would want to know about how my personal goals and plans had changed. My responses led him to demonstrate how changes to my financial plan might better suit me, i.e. he demonstrated the differential value of his recommendations. Of course, there would always be consequences of my decisions, i.e. negative value. Finally he would give me the price of choosing the better path. Carl helped me build a financial portfolio that served me well for a long time.*

MANAGING THE BUYING PROCESS

In most cases the purchase of technology services is a group effort. So if we are going to effectively present the value and price, we need to do that to more than one person. Managing the buying process is the activity of effectively making your value case broadly to all involved in the purchase decision.

Virtually every sales system focused on major B2B sales recommends an in depth look at the parties involved in the purchase decision and their role. The relevance for pricing could not be clearer. If our ability to capture price is contingent on communicating value, then we need think about the details of value communication.

The roadmap for thinking about how to engage the customer's organization is the buying process. For this sale, in this company, at this time, what are the steps in the buying process? Typically your champion will lay it out for you. This is the timing. These are the steps. These are the people. These are their roles. These are the requirements. Etc. Etc. Essentially there are three questions you want to answer

1. What is the customer's process for selecting a service and supplier?
2. Who are the decision makers who control each of the stages in the process?
3. What is the objective of our interaction with each decision maker / influencer?

Note that decision makers change with the buying situation. Selling a product with a warranty might be one set of decision makers, selling an extended warranty might well be a different set. Making the second or third extended warranty sale may be an individual.

For each decision maker, we want to have a plan of attack. We have done the work of understanding how our offering impacts the customer's business. Now is the time to put that information to use. The challenge is that different people in the purchasing process have different concerns. For example, The Sales VP, CIO and Purchasing Director all have different concerns when it comes to purchasing services related to a CRM. So the value drivers that each cares about are going to be somewhat different. Earlier we talked about the importance of incentives to sales behavior. Well, same holds true for decision makers. Understanding how each decision maker is rewarded or punished directly relates to what they care about.

Once you know who the players are and what they care about it is time to build your "treasure map". How many movie adventures begin with a map? The classics are the Indiana Jones movies, especially the one that revolves entirely around his father's book – the roadmap to the Holy Grail. Our map pairs value drivers with decision makers. In other words: What is the value case we need to make to the various parties in the decision making process? The table below illustrates what we are after.

Value Drivers	VP Marketing	VP Operations	VP Finance	VP Procurement
	Mariah Carey	Madonna	Beyonce	Lady Gaga
Faster Product Development	X			
Reduced COGS		X	X	X
Access to Technical Support		X		X
Consulting Support	X			X

Of course, you can build this out to include the entire purchase process, including specific actions to take with each person, and a scorecard. This approach let's you see if there are any important gaps in your value communication process and well enable you to more powerfully make the case for your price.

NEGOTIATE TRADEOFFS

If you have been reading for a while, and are a bit tired, I would like you to put this aside and do something else to refresh yourself. Take a power nap or jump on a treadmill, or walk your dog, or yell at your kids. Whatever it is I want you wide awake for the next few pages.

To start I want to remind you that we set the stage for our ability to negotiate tradeoffs as part of our offering design work in pricing strategy. Unless you have a price menu that permits you to trade off options with your customer, based on both value delivered and your costs, then your sales directors' ability to negotiate will be constrained. Price menu development needs to be done in advance in the case of structured offerings and proactively during the sales process with unstructured offerings.

The process of negotiating tradeoffs actually begins with the buyer profile work we did at the beginning of the chapter. I started this chapter with buyer profiles because that should be work done early on in the sales process. That work informs the sales and pricing process and culminates in negotiation strategies. So we are closing this chapter by coming back to it. Now let's walk through each profile and talk about sales and negotiation strategies for each.

NEGOTIATING WITH PRICE BUYERS

Remember the two parts of the price buyer mantra: We want your lowest price and our requirements are minimal. Success in negotiations begins by listening to what they are saying. They are unwilling to pay for your differentiation. They are unwilling to pay for a relationship. They don't care. They have well defined requirements. So your initial offer to them is a basic offer that meets their minimal requirements and is low cost to you. Your goal is to make good margins even if the services required and price are low. In other words your first step is to meet them where they are.

The second step with price buyers is to test the possibility that they may want more. This is where your ala carte menu comes into play. Price buyers are often highly price sensitive on the core offering, but may be much less price sensitive when it comes to ancillary services. Maybe they desperately need a certain kind of technical support. Maybe throughput is critical, and shutdowns cost them millions per hour. Your job is to probe for these as incremental sales opportunities.

Of course these buyers will push to have these services included. Here is where you need to draw the line. Your differentiation is in these services. The two biggest dangers you face with price buyers are selling at a loss and losing your price integrity on your high value services. So price your core offering as competitively as you feel is necessary

> *The two biggest dangers you face with price buyers are selling at a loss and losing price integrity on your high value services. Price your core offering competitively, but protect your family jewels.*

to win at a profit, but protect the family jewels. If these buyers really need them, then they will prove themselves not to be wholly price buyers. There is some value buyer in them.

Finally, don't get sucked into a bidding war. Decide your lowest profitable price, go with it at the outset, and stick with it. They asked for your best price at the outset. Don't disappoint them. Price buyers are sharks. You don't need to chum the water. If you see a feeding frenzy materializing, get out of the water. If you need to occasionally walk away from a deal, so be it. Better that than getting stuck in a customer relationship that sucks the profitability out of your company.

In closing, these buyers want your best price for a minimal acceptable offering. They say they don't want value and don't want a relationship. Take them at their word. If during the course of the sales process they decide differently, then they pay like everybody else.

NEGOTIATING WITH VALUE BUYERS

By contrast, value buyers are obsessing over your family jewels. Their mantra is "we want your value at a competitive price". In other words, value buyers are looking for services that can have a meaningful and significant impact on their business. They are going to do their homework and shop around. If you have the differential value they are looking for, they are willing to pay a fair price for it.

What kind of negotiating strategy do you want with a value buyer? Remember the second Matrix movie, *Matrix Reloaded*? In the opening sequence Trinity rides a motorcycle off the roof of a skyscraper and drops it on top of a security building, destroying it with a flair that only Hollywood could manifest. She then elegantly dispenses with a host of rent-a-cops, and marches into the heart of the enemy's fortress to save Neo's mission. That's the attitude you need in selling to value buyers. You need to demonstrate your value and keep hammering away at it. Value buyers care about both value and price. If you don't demonstrate value they will devolve into price buyers.

> *Value buyers care about both value and price. If you don't demonstrate value they will devolve into price buyers.*

So you need to explain your value, demonstrate your value and document your value. Focus on the 2 or 3 things they really care about. Your goal is to show the buyer that yours is the best solution for their requirements. It may make sense to tailor your offering specifically to their needs using your offering menu. Include services that create value and strip away services that don't. That's the negotiation process. If price pressure emerges, offer to pull out services. See how your buyer responds. What is more important to them: value or price?

You may want to show how the value of their initial investment will grow over time delivering even greater benefits. Your innovation strategy may be quite appealing to them. They will want to see you as a partner in achieving their business objectives. Cover all areas of value – functional, process, relationship and social. Your goal is to discover and fulfill their vision of that partnership, built on value delivery.

In sum, sell value to a value buyer.

Negotiating with Relationship Buyers

The Center for Services Leadership at Arizona State University is the leading academic think tank dedicated to the business of services.[31] Through their research they have drawn an interesting conclusion about customer loyalty. Customer loyalty is strongest at companies where suppliers have made amends for past mistakes. In other words, the supplier screwed up. The supplier admitted they screwed up. The supplier had a conversation with the customer about how to fix the screw up. And finally the supplier fixed the screw up, cementing the relationship. So loyalty is built over time based on experience – good and bad – resulting in a high degree of trust.

Unlike value buyers or price buyers, relationship buyers are investing in that trust. You have my back and I have yours. This is a strategy that helped build IBM. Early in its history, when an IBM product failed, their minions would descend on the customer's location like a platoon of Navy SEALs. Their mission was to solve the customer's problem as expeditiously as possible and made it clear that they had their customer's back. This may very well have been the source of the notion that "nobody ever got fired for hiring IBM".

The first step in negotiating with relationship buyers is to decide if the relationship is with you or a competitor. If they are loyal to a competitor, think

---

[31] http://wpcarey.asu.edu/csl/

long and hard before investing any effort. The likelihood you will win them over is slim to none. If the relationship is with you, then invest in the relationship.

Relationship buyers are willing to buy what you recommend. They trust you, so offer bundled solutions and reward long term commitments. Reinforce the idea that there is value is doing business with you. This might be American Express's intent when they say "membership has its privileges".

> *Relationship buyers trust you, so offer bundled solutions and reward long term commitments.*

That said, don't neglect functional value. My suggestion is that your treat your relationship buyers like value buyers, but toned down a bit and with that little something extra. If price issues emerge, offer to withdraw services from the bundle. Gauge their response and go from there.

NEGOTIATING WITH CONVENIENCE BUYERS

Recall that the mantra of convenience buyers is "we want it all and we want it now". By definition, convenience buyers are short on time. So the key to successful negotiations is speed of resolution. They don't have time to shop around. They want a solution that works for its purpose and are willing to pay for the convenience. So give them what they want. In this case process value trumps functional value and relationship value.

Sometimes solving a convenience buyer's problem lends itself to a systematic solution. Let's say you have a customer who periodically needs accelerated response, i.e. they are periodically a convenience buyer. Then the solution is to incorporate that service element into a contract with pre-negotiated terms. When the need arises, you have handled it as conveniently as could be imagined.

FORCING VALUE TRADEOFFS

Why do sales people believe price buying is on the rise? The answer is that customers have found that behaving like price buyers works. Loyalty to suppliers can be expensive. Professional negotiators, i.e. procurement, find it is in their best interest to ignore value. Some have not experienced the costs of pure price buying. Others aren't aware of the value of buying value. Others just use their position to further the interests of their companies.

That said, we as sales people are complicit. Too often we don't understand value delivered, and so can't sell it. Our sales and marketing efforts are feature based. We reward customers for their aggressive negotiating tactics by discounting our services. We pay people to sell, but not for price performance or margin. At the end of the quarter, we panic and take what we can get.

To deal with these aggressive tactics, we need new rules for negotiation. These rules are intended to force the customer to reveal their value nature.

1. Before discussing price with the customer, establish value by building a value estimate and communicating it to the customer.
2. Never talk about price in isolation. Only discuss price relative to value delivered.
3. Negotiate tradeoffs with the customers, not concessions from you.
4. Force value and relationship buyers to feel the pain of loss. Pull elements out of the offering in response to demands for a lower price.

5. Likewise force price buyers to feel the pain of loss. Give them what they want, but then remind them of what they are missing.

In sum, effective negotiation begins with the first customer encounter in diagnosing their buying behavior. That diagnosis will tell you how to manage the sales situation to optimize price capture. Your ability to capture price is directly related to your ability to communicate value. With value or relationship buyers, demonstrate value and take stuff away in response to price pressure. With price buyers, demonstrate your willingness to meet their price and then show them what they are missing.

> *What is forcing change? Global competition. What works succeeds; what doesn't is penalized. Please feel free to hold on to your economic, political, social and moral philosophies. If they make you effective, you'll prosper – if not, you'll suffer. No country or company is immune. I'm not saying this is good or bad . . . It just is.*
>
> . . . .
>
> *The implications to the sales role is that you must help your client succeed. If you do, you both win. If not, you both lose. That's a big switch. It is no longer sufficient to get them to buy. If you can't reduce their costs; increase revenues or margins; leverage their cost of capital; increase productivity, quality, and customer satisfaction; augment a key strategy or initiative; and increase critical performance, you cannot earn their business over time.*
>
> . . . .
>
> *As a business person, I can't afford to give business to Fred because he is my golf partner. I can't stand pat with XYZ just because I've done business with them for 10 years. I don't have a lot of time for chitchat and sales pitches, or poorly designed schemes. Let's cut to the chase and cut through the nonsense. Let's get real.*
>
> *Mahan Khalsa, Let's Get Real or Let's Not Play*

"Not long ago, a guy here did an analysis of our pricing in appliances and found out that about $5 billion of it is discretionary. . . . It was the most astounding number I have ever heard – and that's just in appliances. Extrapolating across our business, there may be $50 billion that few people are tracking or accountable for. We would never allow something like that on the cost side."

- Jeff Immelt

CHAPTER 9 - PRICING INFRASTRUCTURE

Most of the people reading this could probably run rings around me on the subject of infrastructure. I mean, that's what tech companies do – provide the infrastructure that companies run on. More, every company is different so a specific recommendation might be overkill in one situation and wholly inadequate in another. My goal in this chapter is, for the most part, to cover the basics.

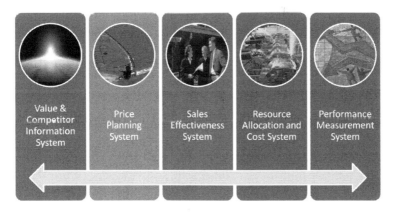

The exception is price performance measurement. I am going to go into some detail on that topic because it is near and dear to my heart and an automatic way to get to better pricing behaviors, leading to almost immediate pricing results.

VALUE AND COMPETITOR INFORMATION SYSTEM

If you are going to sell value, you need to understand value and apply it in your day to day decision making. So you need a value information system. To quote an earlier passage: "Value based pricing goes for the jugular. This is not mamby pamby marketing mumbo jumbo. This is: How much money can I make for my customer? How can I convincingly demonstrate that so they acknowledge the value? How much is a fair share for me to keep? How do I structure the deal to force the customer to pay for value delivered?"

The place to start is making some decisions about who is responsible for thinking about value. The system might include business wide frameworks for conceptualizing and communicating value. One company I am familiar with uses VBS Mapping to routinely make the connection between value drivers, benefits and offering attributes in their business. They do it automatically. It is part of their culture. Here is an example VBS Map.

Value-Benefits-Service (VBS) Map

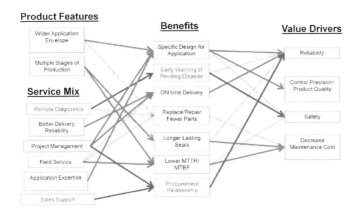

Product Features
- Wider Application Envelope
- Multiple Stages of Production

Service Mix
- Remote Diagnostics
- Better Delivery Reliability
- Project Management
- Field Service
- Application Expertise
- Sales Support

Benefits
- Specific Design for Application
- Early Warning of Pending Disaster
- ON time Delivery
- Replace/Repair Fewer Parts
- Longer Lasting Seals
- Lower MTTR/ MTBF
- Procurement Relationship

Value Drivers
- Reliability
- Control Precision/ Product Quality
- Safety
- Decrease Maintenance Cost

Using this kind of mapping, the company has a united vision of how it creates value for its customers. Over time value drivers, benefits and attribute priorities will change. In the example above, for instance, remote diagnostics had come to the fore as a result of industry events. Finally, your value information system needs to inform your annual planning process and integrate marketing, sales and service engineering efforts.

Like value information, competitor information is vital to good pricing. As organizations grow they often develop quite sophisticated competitor intelligence databases. As with the value system, competitor information changes over time. It is used everywhere from the business planning process, to the offering design process, and during sales and negotiations.

An important consideration of competitor information is getting the information to those who need it when they need it. I was working with a large telecomm firm and met with the VP of Sales. During our conversation he

213

mentioned that one of the real challenges he had was getting good accurate and timely competitor information. A bit later the same day I was meeting with a product manager. During this conversation the manager bragged about how good his competitor information was. He was meticulous about gathering and updating his competition database. When I asked him where he kept the information he responded it was on his PC.

PRICE PLANNING SYSTEM

During your annual business planning process and in developing new offerings, don't forget proactive price planning. Effective pricing strategy is the integration of offering design and pricing. So the organization needs a systematic way to maintain good pricing as the service portfolio grows or changes as the case may be.

My suggestion is that the organization use a formal process to make sure the bases are covered. More, this should be at the front end. Price drives behavior of customers, competitors, sales and channels. What behaviors are you trying to drive? Do your price levels and structures do that?

SALES EFFECTIVENESS SYSTEM

CRM systems have brought incredible productivity to sales and marketing organizations, permitting unheard of collaboration to sales people, their managers and marketers around the world.

When I refer to a sales effectiveness system here, I am referring to the pricing system that produces and delivers quotes to sales. It is the system for controlling the re-quoting process as well. It is the system that anchors the policies and authorities of the pricing process. It is the system that permits timely decisions during negotiations. It is the system that facilitates timely evaluation of the economic consequences of decisions both for business leaders and sales people.

So compared to the value and competitor systems which are relatively slow moving and repositories of information, the sales system is fast moving and concerned with communication and manipulation of information.

RESOURCE ALLOCATION AND COST SYSTEM

An important part of service offering design, most pronounced in professional services, is resource allocation. Getting the right people to the right place in the right time in the right way can make the difference between making and losing money in services. Delivery of good value permits higher prices.

The pricer also needs to understand costs. Good offering design and resource allocation both have cost implications. The understanding of cost behavior permits effective negotiations with clients in which margins are maintained, though revenues or offering mix may change.

PERFORMANCE MEASUREMENT SYSTEM

If you want to quickly improve your financial performance, start thinking about pricing like an accountant. For those of you like me that went through accounting in business school with your eyes closed, here is what I mean. Consider the way accounting looks at the cost side of the business. They have every single item the company spent money on categorized and filed. You can ask accounting for a report of travel expenses over the last 3 years, your payables backlog, or the cost of copy paper for your department, and bingo it miraculously appears. Unfortunately, accounting does not keep track of pricing information with the same diligence in most cases.

Actually, that is OK. Accountants would go bonkers in the pricing world. Accountants have well defined rules and track things to the penny. For pricing, our goal is not accounting accuracy. Rather our goal is reasonably accurate measurement in sufficient detail that permits us to understand what is going on most of the time. To that end managers need to build a database of transaction information as described in the table below. That database is then used to produce periodic reports and permit occasional deep dives to address pricing challenges.

As a word of caution, do not underestimate the power of this information. In my experience, companies routinely underestimate the size of the gap, for example, between list price, contract price and pocket price. Let's say you have a 33% operating margin on your $100M service portfolio. Further, let's say the gap between list and pocket prices is 5% higher than you think it is. That 5% represents $5M in lost revenue, or 15% lost margin. Because pricing deals with percents of revenues, even a minor improvement yields substantial financial benefits.

PRICING DATABASE CONTENT

Let's talk about the elements of data, how they might be used, and then look at some example analyses.

Pricing Database Content

Information	Source
Deal Demographics Client name, date, associated product or MSA, sales person, etc.	Contract, customer record or master service agreement
List Price Original quote from the rate card or price sheet or calculator (excluding policy discounts)	Pricing/Quoting department
Value Tradeoffs Offering components removed in exchange for a price concession	Requests for re-quote
Policy Discounts E.g. volume discounts, bundle discounts, etc.	Quotes presented to sales
Discretionary Discounts, Reasons and Authority Discretionary price reductions granted during negotiations, why they were granted and who authorized them.	Requests for re-quote
Contract Price Price written on the contract.	Contract
Off-Invoice Items Special discounts or giveaways not costed or priced in the contract	Contract
Pocket Price Calculated end price after Off-Invoice items are accounted for	Pricing policies document

DEAL DEMOGRAPHICS

Deal demographics are essential to understanding what is going on because pricing shortcomings or opportunities are often situation specific. For example, customers may be more price sensitive when services are sold at the time of a product sale. Or services may be discounted more deeply when associated with a particular product. Or some sales people may discount heavily and others may not. Or some clients may be price buyers and others may be value buyers. Long story short, analysis of price performance depends on an understanding of the buying situation.

LIST PRICE

List price gives us the starting point for analysis. Note this is list price before policy discounts like volume discounts are applied. Some firms track list prices after policy discounts are applied, using something like the term "adjusted list price". Unfortunately, this leads to managers or analysts never questioning the adjustments. This class of potentially rich improvements is thus overlooked.

VALUE TRADEOFFS

Value tradeoffs are important because they can reveal opportunities for establishing price policies. If the same value tradeoff occurs repeatedly during negotiations, then this may reveal an opportunity for a policy based option that streamlines the negotiation process, saving everyone involved time and money.

In PS, value tradeoffs may also be known as scope changes. If you are going to accurately track price performance, then differentiating between scope changes and discounting is essential. That is not to say it is easy. Fortunately, we are not interested in accounting accuracy. Rather we are trying to understand what is happening so we can better manage the pricing process.

POLICY DISCOUNTS

Policy discounts are central to pricing in many TS environments. Let's say you have a policy discount for resident consultants that takes 8% off the list rate if the consultant is resident for at least 6 months. Periodically you should be asking yourself some fundamental questions

    1.   What is the purpose of this policy discount?

2. What customers is it targeting?
3. What evidence proves that it works as intended?
4. Is it at the right level?
5. Should it be eliminated?

Policy discounts often have a life of their own and may endure long after the rationale for having them has disappeared.

I was working with a software company and interviewing a product manager. In their case, when two software packages were bundled together the customer was given a 30% discount on the second package. There was some duplication of functionality between the two, so there was some justification for the price break. When I asked why they chose 30%, he couldn't remember. So I asked if customers would balk at only a 20% discount. The product manager did not think customers would. We changed the discount to 20%. A year later there was no change in sales volume, and that 5 minute conversation turned into $600K in revenues.

DISCRETIONARY DISCOUNTS

Discretionary discounts are the crack cocaine of pricing. They may feel good in the moment, but the consequences can be devastating. High levels of discretionary discounts are a strong indicator of weak pricing policies, weak pricing process, ineffective pricing controls and weak incentives to name a few. More, discretionary discounting teaches your customers that there is a reward for being tough negotiators.

The place to start in understanding discretionary discounting is with a Price Dispersion Analysis. The following chart shows the discounting practices of a PS organization that utilizes high degrees of discretionary discounting.

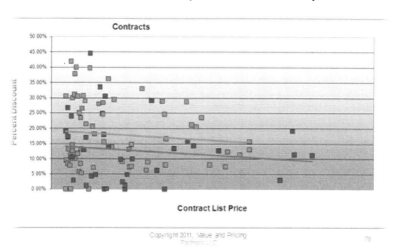

Most executives underestimate the true extent of discounting taking place right under their noses. When I showed this chart to the SVP responsible for the business unit, he practically jumped out of his skin. I am going to clean up the language a bit here, but his commentary went something like this. "Why the hell are our people discounting so highly, in so many cases, damaging the company's margin and their own bonuses?" More, this kind of discounting extends the sales process and literally trains customers to become more aggressive negotiators because they are rewarded for it. This executive proceeded to make changes, reducing discounting by half, thereby adding $4M to the bottom line.

This type of dispersion analysis is useful for answering two types of questions

- Why are some customers willing to pay more for our services than others?
- Why have we sold at such a high discount to some customers?

The answer to these questions may have wide ranging implications for offering design, sales and negotiation strategy.

From a price management standpoint, the goal is to reduce dispersion. As pricers, we cannot talk to our competitors about price, but our customers have no such restrictions. Discounting practices and negotiation strategy are central topics of conversation at procurement conferences worldwide, and you don't want your company to be used as an example. It has been estimated that procurement organizations invest at least 10 times as much in training as business organizations invest in teaching their people how to effectively capture price.

To get the quickest bang for the buck in evaluating price dispersion, I suggest looking for explanations in the following places.

1. Dispersion often varies widely across sales territories or even across individual sales people. Identify the worst offenders and start denying discounting requests. Produce a discounting report by salesperson and territory, and share it with sales management. Let the data speak for itself, and don't broadcast findings. This is potentially embarrassing information and should be held close to the vest.

2. Dispersion often varies by customer. In biblical terms, some "have had their way with you". For the worst offenders, you want to plan a

price migration strategy to raise prices. For others you may want to limit access to services in order to improve margins. For me the bottom line is that it is simply not fair for some customers to carry the water for others.

3. Dispersion varies by product. Deep discounting may suggest products or services that are simply priced too high, and customers won't buy at the full price. In the best of cases, the damage is limited to the individual product or service lines themselves. In the worst of cases, the damage drags down prices for an entire deal. In one case, I analyzed deals over a two year period. I observed that deal price dropped nearly 10% when a certain product was included in the mix. Here, by reducing the price of a single product we actually increased overall deal revenues.

To manage discounting we recommend tracking three key elements of data as illustrated in the Discount Management Report below. What were the discounts given? What was the rationale? And who made the decision to grant the discount? Inevitably you will find that discounts are higher than you thought, likely occur for a common set of reasons and are attributable to a select set of managers. This information is the foundation for pricing control.

Compliance:
Discount Management Report

Deal	Client	Date	$ Price	Discount Type	Incremental % Discount	Cumulative % Discount	Approved <=20%	Approved 21%-30%	Approved 31%-40%	Approved >40%
1	BCBS	1/28/2007	$ 1,500,000	Adj. List Price						
		3/29/2007		Strategic Cust	10%	10%	JC			
		7/30/2007		Bundle	12%	22%		RS		
		9/30/2007		EoQ to Close	7%	29%		RS		
		10/20/2007		Competition	10%	39%			TB	
2	WPMM	4/15/2007	$ 750,000	Adj. List Price						
		7/16/2007		Bundle	20%	20%	RR			
		8/17/2007		Competition	10%	30%		LB		
		9/18/2007		EoQ to Close	15%	45%				KE&BB
3	SCoV	6/30/2007	$ 400,000	Adj. List Price						
		8/1/2007		Prev. contract	10%	10%	RR			
		10/2/2007		Bundle	8%	18%	RR			

CONTRACT PRICE

Contract price is the easiest price to track, and the price that goes into the accounting system. Contract price is the day to day barometer of pricing health. This is the price typically tied to sales incentives when there is a price or margin component in compensation. Contract price is also a barometer of pricing integrity. As you manage price over time, this is the price you are likely to monitor most closely. The contract price represents the deal as a whole, and this is a good place to ask the question: What price should we be tracking?

With products or services, contract price is unit price for the product or service. In the case of many products, this is the price per unit sold. In some cases, such as software, it may be the price per user.

If we are talking about professional services or training services, it gets a little more complicated. Are we talking about the contract rate per resource, the average rate captured for the deal, or the price as a whole for an implementation (or other) project? In order of priority, our recommendation is

1. Track the price as a whole for the project. That is what the customer is buying and that is the price that is exchanged for value delivered. This number also correlates to the total costs of resources put into the deal permitting a calculation of planned margin, sometimes the basis for sales compensation.
2. Track the price/rate by resource. The firm needs to understand how much it is actually earning per resource so it can match these rates against costs. In this case we want to attribute prices to human resources, IP and third party outsourced resources.
3. Though some firms track average rate captured, we find this to be a dubious measure. Is a higher rate better than a lower rate? Not from the customer's standpoint. More about this later when we discuss sales incentives.

If we are talking about a maintenance agreement or a field service contract, should we be tracking the % of the product price or the actual price of the service level agreement? In general, we recommend detaching service prices from product prices. The value of services delivered is in most cases independent of the value of the software or hardware it supports. Product prices may vary considerably over time across the life cycle for good reason – value relative to customer needs and competition changes. It is not clear at all that service value changes in the same way at the same time. Experience has shown that service value is often highest at the start of the product life cycle, dips in the middle and then rises again later. For most services, therefore, we recommend tracking the absolute contract price of services.

The one exception is software maintenance. Maintenance is often pegged at a percent of software license prices, with some firms pegging it to list price and some to contract price. In this case we recommend tracking maintenance as a percent of software price.

OFF INVOICE ITEMS

Off invoice items may or may not appear on the contract, but they should be tracked nevertheless. These may include product giveaways, special contract terms, promises of PS resources for a project or promises of future price concessions on products or services. Tracking these items not only involves knowing what they are, but also attributing a cost to them. Giving away a software module is pretty straightforward – what is the typical price that software would sell for in a similar situation with a similar customer? On the other hand, what is the price of a future promised price concession on a product? Here the pricer must make some assumptions and document them.

Understanding the real cost to the firm of these off invoice items can be crucial to sound negotiation strategy. For example, giving away a couple of months of maintenance costs almost nothing. Promising PS resources for a project can be very costly and drive a deal negative before the ink is dry.

POCKET PRICE

Ultimately the price you capture, after all is said and done, is the pocket price. As a my friend George puts it, "You can't take market share to the bank."

"Before you are a leader, success is all about growing yourself. When you become a leader, success is all about growing others."

-   Jack Welch

CHAPTER 10 - PRICING LEADERSHIP

Pricing leadership is the final element of the PTSP System. Perhaps it should be first. After all, business leaders occupy the bridge. They set direction, navigate the course and adapt to changing conditions. My goal here is to answer the question: How can executives encourage good pricing behavior?

On the subject of leadership I will not presume to tell business leaders how to lead their organizations. Rather, this brief chapter is intended to highlight some important areas for executive attention. Then, in closing, I will relate some of my experiences as a VP of Strategic Pricing inside a middle market software and services company.

OBJECTIVES AND STRATEGY

Early in this book I described the pricing belief systems – cost based, market based and value based. Over half of TS organizations practice cost based pricing. If you are going to use pricing to grow more profitably, then investment in market, competitor and value information is essential. So a good first step by executives is to encourage investment in strategic pricing information.

A second suggestion I have for executives is to expect business and marketing plans that demonstrate meaningful competitive advantage. Pricing is reliant on a good offering that delivers business impact to customers. Too often I have seen me-too products and services that don't deliver the goods. If you want to capture higher prices you must deliver higher value.

A third suggestion is a greater focus on profitability as distinct from revenues. Services businesses have high variable costs. As a result, profits are highly susceptible to price. A focus on service profitability will inevitably lead you to better price management.

My fourth suggestion is to anticipate competitor response. In other words, most price wars start unintentionally. Anticipate how the competitor might respond before you make a price move. Price is the easiest marketing move to make and to respond to. It is also the move with the greatest adverse consequences. Respond strategically to competitor threats.

PROACTIVE MANAGEMENT

Number one on my list here is to have price performance as part of your monthly executive briefing book and as part of your board report. Price is too powerful a profit driver not to be given regular executive attention.

Second, enforce price policies. Your price performance reporting should include price governance measures, for example, what percentage of deals closed within price guidelines? Then, when guidelines are not adhered to, enforce consequences.

My next suggestion is to recognize good pricing performance. Executives can go a long way toward better pricing with a little recognition.

Finally, invest in infrastructure. In too many organizations pricing is managed with an excel spreadsheet with automation provided by Sneakernet Systems. How much time is being lost in the day to day operations of pricing management as a result of weak infrastructure?

SALES EXECUTION

When it comes to sales execution, the place to start is for executives to set the expectation that price concessions require customer value tradeoffs.

Second, invest in sales and management training programs in pricing. If you make them action learning or workout programs, then these kinds of programs can deliver real business results.

Finally, practice what you preach. If executives are personally involved in negotiations, they should abide by pricing policies just like everybody else and expect value tradeoffs for price concessions.

LESSONS FROM A PRICING VP

From 2006-2008 I served as VP of Strategic Pricing at a middle market firm selling software and services, TriZetto Group. In the 10 years before I arrived, the firm had grown to $292M, with EBITDA reported of $48M.

In 2005, the CEO brought in a new COO to install more professional management systems. She, in turn, hired me because "we need strategic pricing to improve profitability". So, perhaps the first lesson from my story is that the primary reason companies invest in better pricing is that it directly drives profitability. Before I would take the job, however, I insisted that we tackle sales compensation first. I knew that nothing I did would work as fast as getting sales attention through their variable comp. She agreed with me. So we were off and running.

As you might expect, changing sales comp was a battle from the outset. It wasn't so much resistance to the concept as turf battle. From my perspective, I didn't want ownership. I wanted change. Perhaps that's why I have always been comfortable as a consultant. Over the course of 9 months I just kept pushing and pushing and pushing, and ultimately got a substantial portion of sales' variable comp based on pricing success. Our goal was 50% of variable comp based on price performance. We didn't get all of that, but we did well. So the second lesson is something every little boy or girl knows: If you want a puppy, start by asking for a pony.

Another immediate project was the deep dive into pricing performance. If I was going to provide direction, I needed to know where I was starting from. So our team went back over 3 years, looking at how list prices were generated for every deal. That was a time consuming manual process, but the results were a gold mine. What I found was that discounting was rampant and that the process for controlling price was full of holes. I am not going to tell you what the level of discounting was, but when I reported my findings to executives, my process and findings were audited. They simply could not believe the results. Lesson number 3 is to make sure your analysis is bulletproof, because you are going to take bullets.

In year two, we launched the new sales comp package. As part of the launch, we made several changes to the price quoting process including provided sales with a calculator so they could estimate the impact of pricing changes on their compensation, for example 5% price change, 20% change in compensation. Lesson number 4 is that sales needs to feel the impact of price incentives as they are selling. Discounting slowed immediately. Most surprising was the impact on services. In this case, our incentives were more successful at driving improved service prices than product prices.

With the history work done, I began measuring price performance and reporting it to the Executive Committee and the Board on a quarterly basis. This was pretty simple and rough at the outset, and got better over time. Nevertheless we were able to document millions in price performance improvement annually. Lesson number 5 is that pricing permits you personally to have a demonstrable impact on bottom line performance.

Throughout my tenure, we launched several pricing research projects. One that stands out in my mind is a project to test the validity of one of the value models we had built. Our in-house modeling suggested that the price level for the software should be roughly $2M. The research revealed, however, that prospective customers would be willing to pay $4M, twice as high as we thought. When we shared this with the business unit heads, they figured for sure we were smoking something. The offering would never sell for that. After repeated meetings including all sorts of colorful language, we decided on $800K. On the one hand, you could argue that this was a loss for us, but product management's initial price point was $100K. So the value price was 8X the price point we would have had, had we not done the homework. Lesson 6 is that the value price may be a multiple of the price you will have if you don't do your homework. And the customer still gets a good deal..

By year 3, we were doing a much better job of integrating pricing into the business planning process. Let me illustrate with just a simple question. When revenues are forecast in the plan, is that based on list price, invoice price or pocket price? Often the question is not even raised. So lesson number 7 is that a focus on pricing improves the quality of business plans and forecasts.

By year 3, our price performance measurement system was in full swing. By the 15th of every month, we produced a pricing analysis of every deal and incorporated our findings and analysis into the Executive Committee's briefing book. As a result, we were able to spot troubling trends early and take immediate action. Lesson 8 is that pricing needs to routinely be on the executive agenda.

Finally, I want to describe one more value pricing project. This is for another new offering with an economic value that was mind boggling, and the competition was fragmented. The problem was that at the value price, customers couldn't afford to buy it. So the pricing recommendation was to structure the offering as components that could be bundled to meet the needs of an individual client at a price they could afford. Let them pay the value price over time as they purchased additional components. Lesson 9 is that offering design and pricing go hand in hand.

My tenure ended when the business was acquired by a private equity firm. In the three years I was there we reduced discounting by half, increased revenues by 50% and doubled EBITDA. I can't claim these results as my own. I was part of an outstanding team. But I am confident saying that Strategic Pricing meaningfully contributed to the company's market and financial performance.

"Life is a series of experiences, each one of which makes us bigger, even though sometimes it is hard to realize this. For the world was built to develop character, and we must learn that the setbacks and grieves which we endure help us in our marching onward."

- Henry Ford

CHAPTER 11 - THE PRICING MATURITY MODEL

Price is often one of the most underutilized weapons in the executive's arsenal. When it comes to pricing practice, there is often ample room for improvement. But where should you make the investment? An investment in tactical pricing may make the most sense in one business, and strategic pricing in another. If you are interested in improving pricing practice, how do you know what investments are right for you?

History has shown that organizations generally mature along a well defined path, growing in pricing sophistication, strategic orientation and power to drive profitable growth. The Pricing Maturity Model maps the path, providing insights into steps any organization can take to improve their pricing capabilities.

Before we move on I want to stress that this path is not a fait accompli. Rather, with a determined executive effort a firm can move from cost based to value based pricing in one fell swoop, gaining all the benefits of the move in a span of 2-3 years. Unfortunately, this is best practice, not normal practice.

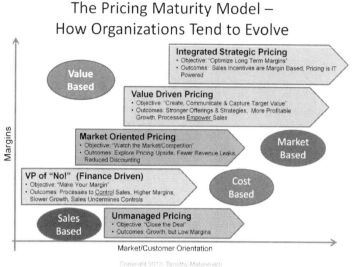

STAGE 1: PRICING IS LARGELY UNMANAGED

As businesses launch, services or otherwise, profitability often takes a back seat to growth and pricing tends to be largely unmanaged. After all, the primary goal of the business is survival, and simply gaining a customer is considered a success. Profitability is generally a function of sales, operating under the belief that if we sell more stuff, we make more money. If there is a pricing philosophy in the firm, it is price to "close the deal". It follows that the organizational locus of pricing power is in the sales organization. As a result, without pricing in the way of sales, the outcome is growth but low margins. Again, for a new business this may not be a bad outcome. It is just not a very profitable outcome.

Over time unmanaged pricing leads to a host of unintended consequences. Lack of profitability ultimately becomes a drag on growth. Pricing practices that closed individual deals become a time consuming and costly contract administration challenge. Inevitably, a deal gets closed that is simply bad for the company and the financial consequences are too great to ignore. More often than not, finance intervenes to save the day. Enter the second stage of pricing maturity: VP of "No!".

STAGE 2: VP OF "NO!"

When finance becomes the locus of pricing authority, the mantra becomes "Make your margin". Pricing controls are established in response to problems. For example, cost overruns on a fixed price contract may have resulted in sizable losses. As a result, price policies and controls are established to limit this risk in the future. In general, during the VP of "No!" stage, there is little thought to aligning price policies with marketing strategies. Pricing and offering structures emerge reactively. While it may not be ideal, it usually works. Margins improve.

Lack of strategic alignment, however, prompts other problems. For a sales force accustomed to pricing flexibility, pricing controls are impediments to closing deals. In order to continue revenue generation, sales proactively works to undermine price controls. It is not malicious intent. Rather it is simply

> *During the VP of "No!" stage margins improve, but there is often little thought to aligning price policies with marketing strategies. The resulting misalignment puts sales and finance at odds, and can lead to increased discounting*

in their best interests to do so. Sales people at this stage are typically compensated on revenues or volume. They are happy to give up 5% or 10% in

237

price to close a deal because it means they still get 90% to 95% of their commissions. There is very little incentive to maintain price integrity.

For the typical American business, however, a 5% price discount can mean a 60% reduction in profitability, and 10% turns profitability into loss, giving financial managers serious heartburn. To make up for it, finance pushes for higher prices, exacerbating an already bad situation. As a result, price discounting increases, but margins are maintained. Pricing integrity and customer relationships suffer the consequences. Customers learn to ignore high list prices and become tougher negotiators. Sales discounting reinforces the behavior. As VP of "No!", finance has improved margins, but often at a price, i.e. increasing irrelevance of list prices.

STAGE 3: MARKET ORIENTED PRICING

As list prices and discounting increase, complaints grow from the sales organization that prices are too high. Truth is that prices may be too high, exactly right or too low, but there is little evidence to support or refute the assertion. Organizations respond, as they should, by looking to the marketplace and profiling competitors and their pricing. The mantra becomes "Match the Market". In the evolution of pricing capability, this is an important step. It is the first step toward a strategic view of pricing where competitor behavior and the role of pricing in creating competitive advantage are considered in decision making. Pricing moves from a being a financial afterthought to a strategic variable in business planning.

On the financial front, pricing tends to grow from a reactive process to a more proactive process. Finance driven pricing analytics emerge to track pricing performance, limit price variance and reduce revenue leaks. Market prices are captured and competitors are profiled to better understand the firm's value and price positioning.

Despite the best of intentions, the stage of market oriented pricing is fraught with risk. Paradoxically, risk may very well increases if competitors choose to match one another's prices. An example illustrates the point. Let's say Acme consulting finds its prices for a system implementation are higher than the competition. Sales argues the price premium is the reason for recent lost sales. Business leaders are concerned with volume, and decide to match the industry average. Of course, the immediate and obvious risk is to profitability because for the typical technology PS practice, there is an 10:1 multiplier from price to profits.

Market oriented pricing may lead to unintended price competition, market disequilibrium and damage the industry's ability to generate earnings.

A subtler, more strategic risk is the potential disruption of market equilibrium due to the rate cut, potentially igniting price competition. This is especially true for large industry players who are in a position to move the market itself. History has shown that most price wars start unintentionally when a competitor disrupts the price-value equilibrium. Case in point, a generic veterinary pharmaceutical business had established itself as a sizable minority player serving the livestock industry. In an effort to improve its market position the firm began offering a free service to its customers: buy $X worth of pharmaceuticals annually, and we will provide you free software and consulting to optimize dosing, livestock yield and the financial impact. It is value selling at its best. Customers loved the services, and the firm's sales began to grow rapidly. Unfortunately there was no value price for the services to go along with this step change in value delivery. To

239

stem share losses, competitors began dropping prices of their products. They could not match value, so they had to drop price. Not understanding that they had caused the problem in the first place, the generics firm misinterpreted the competitor reaction as an aggressive price move. Believing it was mistaken about the value of its new services, it dropped prices in response. And so it went. Two years later, prices were still spiraling down.

The risk is just as great for a firm positioned below the industry average. Let's say the firm's rates are 10% below the industry average and business leaders decide this is a great opportunity to raise PS rates. The real question again is: Price relative to what value delivered? If the firm is perceived by customers as delivering OK value at an OK price, then a rate increase will likely result in lost sales. The industry overall stays healthy, but the firm puts itself in jeopardy.

In sum, closing the price gap in either direction has risks because without corresponding information about value, price moves can result in unintended adverse consequences. In the short run, price too high, you lose business and price too low, you lose margin. In the long run, you may disrupt market equilibrium and damage the industry's ability to generate earnings for years to come.

STAGE 4: VALUE DRIVEN PRICING

Unfortunately, if you are watching the competition you are not watching the customer. That's the problem with market oriented pricing. The unique characteristic of value driven pricing is the primacy of value, where the focus is squarely on the needs and wants of the customer. Professor Jim Anderson at Northwestern defines value as "the worth in monetary terms of the technical, economic, service and social benefits a customer firm receives in exchange for the price it pays". Here's an example to illustrate the difference between market oriented and value driven pricing.

An advertising agency specialized in the development of advertising programs for physicians and attorneys. If you tune into daytime television on a sick day, you have seen their work. Over 20 years they built a brand and set of offerings second to none. A new competitor entered the market, targeting the specific needs of trial attorneys. Why trial attorneys? Because trial attorneys often have incomes several times as high as other members of the legal profession. The new competitor created a set of premium offerings at roughly 5X the price of the existing firm, and successfully established itself as a viable competitor. By focusing on value and willingness to pay, the new entrant created a very profitable beachhead in the market space. Obviously, if the new entrant had focused on the competition instead of value, they likely would have ended up with a mediocre offering and a small market position. The focus on value enabled their successful market entry.

This example illustrates the mantra of the value driven pricer: "Create, Communicate and Capture Target Value".

In their book, *Blue Ocean Strategy,* Kim and Mauborgne describe the primacy of value in the "Strategic Sequence" where value determines price, price determines costs, and costs determine operational investments. The value orientation enables breakthrough offerings and strategies. Price and volume are no longer

> *Value oriented pricing resulted in more satisfied customers, happier employees and higher profitability.*

at odds. Deliver good value at a fair price and profitable growth ensues. One study found that value oriented pricing resulted in more satisfied customers, happier employees and higher profitability. When price and volume are no longer at odds, pricing processes can be configured to empower sales and shorten the sales cycle.

STAGE 5: INTEGRATED STRATEGIC PRICING

For some pricing professionals, value driven and strategic pricing are synonymous. But that is not my experience. Integrated strategic sricing is another step change in organizational pricing maturity primarily characterized by three features.

1. Sales incentives are margin based
2. Value and price positioning are tracked
3. Pricing is IT powered

Strategic pricing is integrated if the CEO and the sales representative are speaking from the same sheet of music. Experience has shown, however, that if sales incentives are not tied in a significant way to margin or a proxy, like price, then sales people will routinely undermine pricing authority and controls.

In my view, sales compensation is the acid test of integrated strategic pricing. In my experience, sales people will in most cases use price discounts to close a deal unless they are paid to do otherwise.

The second criteria for demonstrating integrated strategic pricing is that both price and value positioning are consistently tracked. The reasoning is simple. New products and services often merit huge investments to determine their initial value and positioning. That is, they are priced for value. But just as in physics, when the new offering enters the fray, the market space and competitors within it adapt to the new entrant. Giving new offering developers the benefit of the doubt, the entry price is probably correct the day before launch. Likewise, the price is probably wrong soon after. Because of the sizable impact on revenues and earnings, price is the most dynamic element of the marketing mix. Tracking value and price positioning over time is essential to the strategic management of pricing.

The third criteria for demonstrating integrated strategic pricing is that pricing is IT powered. Consider, for a moment, the accounting system in place for managing costs. Most businesses can tell you to the penny how much they paid for paper clips last year. They do so with the benefit of a sophisticated IT system. Now look at the revenue side of the equation. In many cases a price management information system (PMIS) could go a long way in helping business leaders optimize the revenue generation potential of their businesses. PMIS solutions have been shown to dramatically speed and simplify price management in the following ways.

- Quoting Efficiency & Effectiveness
- Pricing Process Management
  - Policies & controls
- Decision & Negotiation Support
- Price Management
  - Real time business performance relative to plan
- Price Performance Measurement
- Price Planning & Analysis
  - Customer profitability
  - Demand curves & elasticity
- Link to Plans, Forecasts, Pipeline, Backlogs

So the question ultimately is: What level of pricing maturity does your organization exhibit? I'm not saying any level is necessarily good or bad. It just depends on your situation. If you are a relatively new service organization, trying to get your legs, cost based pricing may not be bad. Perhaps the most important consideration for you as a service business is to cover your costs. Over time, service costs will eat your company's lunch so you better do that. In my experience, however, companies carry cost based pricing too far. Data suggests nearly 60% of service organizations – even at middle market or larger companies – use cost based pricing. That's just too high.

If you are a more well developed service organization, then the shift to market based pricing makes sense. Usually it means higher margins for your service business and it provides sales with cover. They need to believe that there is validity to service prices. Market based pricing works best with essential services where there are peers to compare to. So if your services strategy is that of a product provider, then market based pricing may be satisfactory.

If you are shifting to a product extender model from a product provider, or if you are launching value added services, or if you are facing large customers, then the shift to value pricing in services makes sense. Solution provider and systems provider business models also beg for a value based approach. In these cases services are central to your value positioning and frankly you need the profitable growth that services provide. In these cases value pricing creates more upside than the other models.

That said, unless incentives are aligned with pricing or margin performance, your value pricing will be hamstrung. Control systems in pricing work. Incentives, however, will trump controls when the two are in conflict. When you better align incentives, you are making the step toward integrated strategic pricing. You are beginning to manage pricing on a par with other business disciplines.

You may make the change when the realization hits you that you are trying to manage half the revenue side of the business using Excel spreadsheets. For example, you operate in 32 countries. How are you optimizing your global pricing? If you operate gloabally, IT powered pricing makes a lot of sense.

Finally, most price management systems do a great job of measuring tactical pricing performance, but fall short on pricing strategy. The final criteria for integrated strategic pricing is tracking value positioning and value pricing together. Now that's price performance measurement.

Acknowledgements

I claim the words in the book as my own, but truth is I am standing on the shoulders of so many people I have learned from throughout my career.

The place to start is with a thank you to TSIA. It is an outstanding organization, focused on figuring out what works and what doesn't in technology services. Most particularly thanks to Bo DiMuccio, VP of Professional Services. Bo has been a good friend, confidante and co-conspirator. His research has been a wellspring of insights into pricing at professional service organizations. Likewise, I am learning more every day from Julia Stegman who heads up TSIA's revenue generation discipline. Thanks also to Lydia Zaffini, John Ragsdale and Tom Pridham who have made my partnership with TSIA a tangible asset. Thanks to J.B. Wood. J.B. spent hours with me talking about his view of the role of pricing in technology services. Finally, thanks to Thomas Lah who wrote the perfect Foreword.

In terms of pricing mentors, I must start with George Cressman at World Class Pricing. George has been a good friend and mentor for many years. He is the smartest pricer I have ever met. Second would be Irv Gross at ISBM. Irv was a great explainer. I also want to thank my former business partner, Jerry Dozoretz, may God rest his soul. Thanks also to my friends at StratX who taught me how to think strategically and design effective training programs. Anyone reading this can see the influence of pricers, Tom Nagle, Reed Holden and Mike Marn, and value expert Jim Anderson. Finally thanks to Ralph Oliva at ISBM for his friendship over many years.

Of course, thanks to all my clients who have been laboratories for my work and who have inspired me to think creatively about the pricing. In the interest of confidentiality, I will not mention them here.

Personally, two people have helped me maintain my sanity through the process. (Hah! They might argue if I were sane I would have never started this project.) Herb Rubenstein of Sustainable Business Group has been a good friend and counsel. I can't thank him enough. Pamela Herbert believed in me through thick and thin, even when I didn't believe in myself. She encouraged me to free my creative spirit and speak with my own voice.

Thanks to Emelene Russell for her outstanding work on the cover.

Thanks so much to all who read and endorsed my book. If it were not for your encouragement through the process, I may never have finished. You have honored me by taking your valuable time with it. I am forever grateful.

Four books inspired me to write this one. First, Mahan Khalsa's first edition of his book *Let's Get Real or Let's Not Play* was the inspiration, many years ago, for this book. That book was my 60,000 word model of success. Second, *The 4 – Hour Work Week* by Tim Ferriss. That book persuaded me to productize my knowledge as a way to detach earning from hours. Third, The E-Myth Revisited by Michael Gerber. That book taught me the importance of creating a system for addressing a problem, and to be unsatisfied with a patchwork of tools and processes. Fourth, *Consumption Economics* by J.B. Wood, Todd Hewlin and Thomas Lah. That book convincingly demonstrated the changes taking place in the business of tech and cemented the need for this book in my mind. Thank you all.

Thanks to Margaret Matanovich for all she has done to take care of our family when my attention was elsewhere. Thank you to Simon and Eleanore Choppa for their support.

Thanks to Mary Helen and Frank Bolvari for showing me I could open my eyes under water.

Finally there are people who helped me through the process, many not intentionally. I simply must mention them here. Sherry Stedman, Lisa Frederickson, Mike Bronx, Art Crisis, Emily Armbrust, Barrett Blank, Rich Leach, Tony Penna, Angela Libby Jankowski, Emelene Russell, Jim O'Hara, Lisa Holland, Karen Copeland and Erin Vang.

If I have neglected anyone, I apologize sincerely.

About the Author

Timothy Matanovich is speaker, trainer and consultant in pricing. He is currently president of Value and Pricing Partners. From 2006 – 2008 Tim was Vice President, Strategic Pricing and Value at The TriZetto Group. Prior to joining TriZetto, Tim was General Partner at Market Leaders Group, and a Senior Consultant with StratX. Among others, Tim has worked with industry leaders GE, DuPont, Ericsson, PPG, VHA, First Data and Salesforce.com.

Tim has been an adjunct faculty member with the Institute for Study of Business Markets at Penn State, the Center for Services Leadership at Arizona State, the American Marketing Association and at TSIA. Tim received his MBA from the University of Michigan, and makes his home in Colorado.

Value and Pricing Partners (www.valueandpricing.com) recently received the coveted *Recognized Innovator Award for Excellence in Consulting Services* from the Technology Services Industry Association (www.tsia.com).

To book Tim as a speaker or trainer, or for more information about how better price management can benefit your organization, call 303-526-9084 or email Tim at tim@valueandpricing.com .

A Personal Note

We are privileged to spend our days thinking about business management issues like pricing. Many around the world, however, face more pressing questions like: Where am I going to sleep tonight? What kind of life will I have without the limbs I lost in the war? When will my hurricane ravaged community recover? Please don't forget to open your heart, and your wallet, to those in need. Thank you.

Tim Matanovich